Your Christian Wedding

The complete handbook
for planning

Your Christian Wedding

Kay Oliver Lewis

FLEMING H. REVELL COMPANY
OLD TAPPAN, NEW JERSEY

Library of Congress Cataloging in Publication Data

Lewis, Kay Oliver.
   Your Christian Wedding.

   Bibliography: p.
   1. Weddings — United States — Handbooks, manuals,
etc. 2. Marriage — United States. I. Title.
II. Title: Your Christian wedding.
HQ745.L48   392'.5   81-1226
ISBN 0-8007-1259-5   AACR2

TO
my *loving husband,*
Tom,
without whom none
of this would have
been possible

Contents

Preface

You're engaged! Congratulations and best wishes!

Your wedding is one of the most important events in your life. You probably already have visions of what you'd like. But the decisions and details can seem overwhelming at first. No doubt you wonder, "Where do I begin?" and "How will I get everything done?"

That's what I wondered when I first became engaged. A friend came to my rescue with a checklist of what needed to be done, and in what order. She showed me her notebook in which she had planned her wedding. Using that as a basis, I wrote my more detailed list and began a planning notebook.

My goal was to complete everything the week before the wedding so I could enjoy the big day. That meant being calm and relaxed with nothing to do besides get dressed and pack a few last items for the honeymoon. Although that goal seemed impossible when the pace got hectic, the planning notebook came to my aid. Because I had outlined each detail in the order in which it needed to be completed, nothing was missed. The result: a joyful wedding with a minimum of confusion—and a happy bride!

This book is written to help you enjoy your wedding and all the work and planning that goes into it. Just follow the instructions one at a time, and you can plan your perfect wedding with a minimum of confusion.

As important as your wedding day is, it lasts only a day. Your marriage lasts "as long as you both shall live." Planning your marriage, therefore, is much more important than planning your wedding. You'll want to care for all the details of your wedding day, of course. But never allow those details to eclipse your relationship. The flowers will wilt, and the cake will be eaten. But the patterns you begin as you make your wedding decisions together will become the foundation of your marriage. How you make each decision is more important than the decision itself. Can you harmonize your ideas, compromising where necessary? Are you considerate of each other? Can you handle anger and stress? If so, you are doing something much more important than planning a wedding. You're building the foundation for a happy marriage.

"Marriage is instituted by God." You've heard that line at many weddings. As you contemplate your own marriage, this truth increases in importance. You look ahead and wonder whether your marriage will last. Will you be able to cope with unforeseen stresses? Will you continue to love each other and to grow together?

You know the statistics all too well. But your marriage can last. Why? Because marriage is instituted by God. He has given you every resource through His Word and His Spirit. Whatever the trials you will meet, He has already promised, "My grace is sufficient" (*see* 2 Corinthians 12:9). The eternal God is for you and for your marriage. He will never leave you or forsake you. He has promised to be your refuge and your strength, a very present help in trouble (*see* Psalms 46:1).

Marriage is the oldest institution on earth. In the beginning, when God created the heaven and the earth, God saw that His work was good. When He created man, behold, it was *very* good. One thing, however, was not good. God said, "It is not good that the man should be alone; I will make a helper fit for him" (*see* Genesis 2:18). So from the rib of man, God made woman and brought her to the man. "Then the man said, 'This at last is bone of my bones and flesh of my flesh. . . .' Therefore, a man leaves his father and his mother and cleaves to his wife, and they become one flesh" (Genesis 2:23, 24 RSV).

God instituted marriage to insure man's complete happiness. Soon after that perfect wedding, however, sin forced Adam and Eve's exit from the Garden. Sin also marred their marriage. No longer could each enjoy a perfect mate.

God did not abandon Adam and Eve in their sin, but promised a Saviour. Nor did God abandon the idea of marriage. Throughout Scripture He exalts the institution He began in Eden.

God celebrates the union of man and woman in the Song of Songs. Whatever your interpretation of this book, one thing is certain. The two lovers extol their love and sexual relationship. And He calls their flowery phrases inspired! As the Author of marriage, He wants your romance to be equally rapturous.

In the Song of Songs, God describes love as ". . . The very flame of the Lord. Many waters cannot quench love, Nor will rivers overflow it . . ." (Song of Solomon 8:6, 7, 8 NAS). This is the love God has designed for you.

Jesus Christ adorned marriage with His presence and first miracle at Cana in Galilee (*see* John 2). He not only approved of the festive occasion, but made it better by supplying quality wine in abundance.

The inspired Word teaches that marriage is honorable (*see* Hebrews 13:4), and Paul compares the relationship of husband and wife with that of Christ and His Church (*see* Ephesians 5:22–33).

One day in heaven believers in Christ will join in the greatest celebration of all: the marriage supper of the Lamb. Before planning your wedding, read about that glorious wedding in Revelation 19 where God announces, "Hallelujah! For the Lord our God, the Almighty, reigns. Let us rejoice and be glad and give the glory to Him, for the marriage of the Lamb has come and His bride has made herself ready. . . . Blessed are those who are invited to the marriage supper of the Lamb" (Revelation 19:6, 7, 9 NAS).

You have been invited to that celebration, for Christ says, ". . . let the one who is thirsty come; let the one who wishes take the water of life without cost" (Revelation 22:17 NAS).

This book is written to help you get ready for your wedding day. But first we hope you will be ready for that greatest marriage celebration. Those who place their faith in the Lord Jesus Christ, trusting His shed blood to cleanse all their sin, can know not only the joys of married love here on earth, but will also spend all eternity celebrating the love of Christ the Saviour.

May your wedding be a reflection of that great celebration. May the God of love bless your wedding with His presence.

Your Christian Wedding

1
Telling the World

What could be a happier announcement than "We're engaged!"? Your friends and family will want to join the fun and add their best wishes. Before the word slips out through the grapevine, think together about making the announcement a special time.

Your parents, of course, will be the first to know. Perhaps you have already followed the time-honored custom of asking their blessing. Whether or not they suspect the big news, honor them with the first announcement. Tell them in person if possible. Thank them for the contributions to your lives that have prepared you for each other.

Your wedding is a family affair. Not only does it unite you to each other, but it also brings your two families together. Begin good relationships with both families by being considerate. Your fiancé's mother will appreciate a thoughtful note expressing your joy in joining her family. If you wish, send a small bouquet of flowers.

Have the two families met? If possible, arrange for the groom's family to pay a friendly, informal call on the bride's family. If this is not possible, tell your prospective in-laws about your own family to help them get acquainted. Give the groom's mother your family's name, address, and telephone number so she can express her happiness if she wishes.

Parents of the bride-to-be might wish to follow tradition

by giving an engagement party for relatives and close friends of both families. If not, the two of you might want to give your own party. Use your ingenuity to make your announcement a surprise in a way that expresses your personalities.

Some newspapers still include engagement announcements. If you wish your news to make the news, send your announcement to the papers in both your hometown and your fiancé's. Some papers provide forms for this information. If they don't, give your name, your fiancé's name, names and residences of both sets of parents, short biographical material on both of you (such as schools from which you graduated and present jobs), and the expected date of your wedding. You can send an eight-by-ten black-and-white glossy photograph. Write your identification on a separate paper and tape it to the photo. Note, however, that even if not used, this photograph will not be returned.

2
The Planning Begins

When you first become engaged, the decisions ahead seem endless. And it seems they all must be made at once! When and where will the wedding take place? How many guests can be invited? Where will the reception be held? Who will officiate? Who will be the attendants?

Before you panic and elope, take courage. You don't have to make every decision today. So relax and take one thing at a time.

Consider the Type of Celebration

First, what type of wedding do you want? Think together about your values and your tastes, and plan a celebration that will feel comfortable to you. Keep in mind that weddings do not belong solely to the bride, but also to the families. Therefore, consider the feelings of others. If your plans would offend a close family member, look for a compromise that will strengthen family ties.

Here are some wedding options you might consider:

Home wedding: This intimate setting provides a warm, comfortable atmosphere for a small group of relatives and close friends. You might feel more relaxed, especially if you enjoy small groups more than crowds. And the service can be worshipful and Christ honoring. His presence is not limited to the church sanctuary, for He promises to be wher-

21

ever "two or three are gathered together" in His name.

A home wedding can be simple, eliminating much of the work associated with larger ceremonies. Costs can be reduced. And the strain on bride and groom is lessened, leaving the two of you more relaxed to begin your honeymoon.

The disadvantage, of course, is that your guest list must be limited to the number that can comfortably fit in the home.

Small chapel wedding: If a church setting is important to you (or your home is too small to accommodate a wedding), but you want only family and close friends, consider getting married in a small chapel or small room of your church decorated for the occasion. You will probably be able to accommodate a few more guests than you would in a home, yet the service will still be intimate. Expense and strain on the bride and groom can be kept to a minimum.

Outdoor wedding: Perhaps you dream of getting married in a garden or other scenic setting. If so, you are in good company. The first wedding, performed by God Himself, took place in a garden.

A garden wedding can be as formal or informal as you wish, and floral decorations are already provided. It will take a bit of extra work to arrange seating and to plan the music with either stringed instruments or recorded selections. But your biggest concern will be the weather. Even if you live in a desert where sunny days are nearly guaranteed, make alternate plans just in case.

Church wedding: A church sanctuary provides an impressive background for a wedding ceremony. It has added significance because you associate the sanctuary with corporate worship. And it has other advantages: a quality organ, good acoustics, a longer aisle, a platform that easily accommodates the wedding party and floral arrangements, and more seating for guests.

Before making your decision, consider a few drawbacks. If your guest list is small, the sanctuary could look empty. A larger event will require more preparation and involve more details. And costs, if not watched closely, can soar. Furthermore, if either of you gets tense or keyed up by large events, the escalated excitement of a full-scale church wedding could prove overwhelming. If either time or budget is sharply limited, this type of elaborate ceremony might prove more taxing than enjoyable.

Know yourselves and your values, then plan the setting where you will feel most comfortable. This is your day to remember, so plan wisely. If you are satisfied and enjoy your service, your guests will enjoy it also.

Whatever your setting, a wedding should be, first of all, a worship service. You will want it to be a reverent reflection of your faith in Christ and your praise to the Creator who calls men and women together in marriage.

Meeting With Your Pastor

Your pastor will want to help you plan a service that worships the God of love. Because he has officiated at many weddings, his counsel can both guide you and save you wasted efforts. Meet with him soon after your engagement.

During your first meeting with the pastor, you will want to discuss with him your decision to marry. If he has any hesitation or biblical injunctions about your union, listen carefully. He is not trying to squelch your joy, but as God's servant, he is trying to guide you into a deeper and more lasting joy by helping you find God's will.

If your pastor affirms your belief that this marriage is God's will, you will want to set the wedding date. Suggest a preferred date as well as alternatives, depending on his schedule and the church calendar. If you are reserving a separate reception site, be prepared to be flexible in setting the date. Also set a date and time for the rehearsal.

During this first meeting with the pastor, let him explain

the church's restrictions on wedding arrangements. These restrictions are usually designed to insure that the service honors Christ rather than elevates the couple or promotes romanticized ideals of love.

Questions to Ask Your Pastor

Some questions you will want to ask:

Does the minister have a set form of service that must be followed, or are we allowed to make some modifications?

Does a specific group in the church handle the reception details? If so, what services do they provide? How much advance notice do they need? And how is payment handled?

Are there guidelines for the music?

Are there any restrictions in decorating the sanctuary or church parlors?

Are there any restrictions concerning who may or may not participate in the ceremony?

What supplies are available from the church? Kneeling benches? Candelabra? Aisle runners? Punch bowls? Coffee pots? Is there a fee?

Is there a fee for using the sanctuary? Church parlors?

Are there standard fees paid to the pastor, custodian, organist, and so on?

Are there any rules concerning wedding photography?

Are facilities available for the bridal party to use for changing clothes? Can these rooms be locked?

During this first meeting, set the dates for premarital counseling. These should begin as early in your engagement as possible for two reasons. First, you will have more time to consider thoughtfully your pastor's advice and make any necessary adjustments in your relationship. Second, your calendar will become increasingly busy as your wedding day nears. Setting these counseling dates establishes your priority to place your relationship above the social flurry.

Premarital Counseling

Whether given by your minister or a professional marriage counselor, premarital counseling is one of the wisest investments you can make. For you are not only planning a wedding, you are planning a lifetime of marriage. Although you won't learn everything about marriage in four to eight counseling sessions, you will gain valuable insights that will start you on the right path.

A good counselor will have a few questions, then will allow you to do much of the talking. He or she will help you resolve potential problems, or help you see where your ideas of marriage are unrealistic. He may give you some tests to reveal your strengths and weaknesses. You'll gain a deeper understanding of yourselves and your relationship. The *Taylor-Johnson Temperament Analysis* is especially useful. It reveals nine personality traits, and shows you not only how you see yourselves but also how you see each other. There are no right or wrong answers—just insights.

Expect the counselor to cover these areas of marriage: values and expectations, husband/wife roles, communication, finances, time management, family relationships, sex, and spiritual growth. He may cover other areas as well.

You'll probably find that these sessions spark further discussion, and help the two of you to know each other even better.

3
Your Wedding Calendar

Once your date is confirmed, you are ready to organize your wedding calendar.

You may have envisioned your engagement days as a constant romantic glow. You will have those days. But you'll also discover that although a wedding is fun and joyous, it is also work. Some days, in fact, it will seem all work and no fun. Every bride feels this way at one time or another. Relax and give yourself a break, and the romantic glow will return.

The work is much easier if you have a list of jobs to be completed, the order in which they need to be done, and suggested deadlines. With this list you will feel organized. And you won't have to worry about arriving on your wedding day having forgotten the napkins or the matches to light the candles. For an event this complicated, organization is the key to success.

The list which follows gives more details than you will probably need. Tailor the list to fit your preferences and your pocketbook. Cross out and forget items that don't apply to you. The list already looks more manageable, doesn't it? As you think of details unique to your wedding, add them in the blank spaces. Then you can be confident that everything is under control.

Pacing Yourself

I know brides who attempted too much that final week and were exhausted before their weddings—and too exhausted to enjoy their honeymoons. So eager was I to avoid that fatigue that I worked like a mad Trojan during the first weeks of engagement. During every break and lunch period I was telephoning for prices and looking up addresses for my card file. Every evening I filled with planning and projects. The result? Exhaustion struck early!

I learned the hard way to pace myself. Given the choice, I'd rather wear out early in the game and have time to recover than to burn out near the wedding. But wise planning can help you avoid exhaustion altogether. You can do it. That's why the calendar includes reminders to relax. Purposefully plan days or at least evenings when you *won't* work on the wedding.

Extra time spent in the early planning and organizing will pay off as the pace increases. Because you know what you must do and when you must do it, there will be a minimum of confusion. And because every detail is listed in one place, you can easily spot anything that has been overlooked.

The work sheet suggests who is responsible for each task according to tradition. But this is not a rigid rule. All that matters is that you agree on who should do what.

The chart also suggests a general time frame for completing each task. If you can finish some jobs earlier, all the better. The less you leave until the last few weeks, the more relaxed you will be.

This calendar lists details for planning the wedding. But remember your marriage is more important than your wedding. You will want to plan time together to discuss your ideas for your home and your roles. If you have not done so, begin now to study the Bible and pray together. Your pastor will be glad to recommend a study plan. When your wedding day arrives, you'll be ready not only to walk the aisle, but ready to walk together through life.

Wedding Calendar

Person Responsible	Task	Due Date	Date Completed
Four to Six Months Before			
Bride and groom	Set wedding date and time.		
Bride and groom	Meet with pastor.		
Bride and groom	Clear date with pastor, church, and reception site.		
Bride and groom	Plan reading/study times together to prepare for marriage.		
Bride, groom, and parents	Discuss wedding budget.		
Bride, groom, and parents	Make guest list.		
Bride and groom	Order wedding rings, and have them engraved.		
Bride	Select bridesmaids.		
Groom	Select best man, ushers.		
Bride and groom	Make card file of guests' names and addresses.		

Person Responsible	Task	Due Date	Date Completed
Bride	Select caterer. Make appointment to discuss final details. Mark date on calendar. Note phone number on service sheet.		
Bride	Select photographer and set date for conference. Note phone number on service sheet.		
Bride	Select florist and set date for a conference about three weeks before the wedding. Note number on service sheet.		
Bride and groom	Select musicians: organist, soloists, others.		
Bride	Shop for wedding clothes: gown, veil, shoes, lingerie.		
Bride and groom	Plan wording of invitations.		
Bride and groom	Select and order invitations.		
Bride	Order other stationery: thank-you notes, informal notes,		

PERSON RESPONSIBLE	TASK	DUE DATE	DATE COMPLETED
	letter paper, napkins (if printed).		
Bride	Plan overall color scheme.		
Bride	Select bridesmaids' dresses and headpieces.		
Bride	Notify attendants to go for measuring and ordering dresses (or give material for sewing).		
Bride and groom	Select china, pottery, crystal, silver, stainless patterns.		
Bride and groom	Decide colors and sizes for table linens (formal and informal), bed linens, bath colors.		
Bride	Register with major department stores in hometowns of both bride and groom. List store numbers on service sheet.		
Bride	Make appointment with gynecologist. List number on service sheet.		

Person Responsible	Task	Due Date	Date Completed
Bride	Begin planning reception: menu		
	room arrangement and serving centers		
	decorations (list any supplies needed)		
	coat racks, if needed		
	check supplies needed for serving:		
	punch bowl		
	coffeepots		
	plates		
	cups		
	silverware		
	napkins		
	tablecloths		
	centerpieces		
	floral arrangements		
Bride	If no caterer is used, engage:		
	hostess		
	kitchen crew		
	cleanup crew		
Bride	Select hospitality committee:		
	guest-book attendant		

Person Responsible	Task	Due Date	Date Completed
	gift receiver		
	servers for reception		
Groom's parents	Plan location for rehearsal dinner (if a restaurant, make reservations).		
Groom	Decide honeymoon plans.		
	Make reservations for: car rental (if necessary)		
	motels		
	plane, train, or bus reservations		
	passports (if required)		
	inoculations (if required)		
Bride and groom	Make dental appointments and have any necessary work done.		
Bride	Check wardrobe. Do any mending or hemming. Discard or give away items not worn in a year.		
	List items to be purchased.		

PERSON RESPONSIBLE	TASK	DUE DATE	DATE COMPLETED
THREE MONTHS BEFORE			
Bride	Begin addressing invitations (allow plenty of time).		
Bride	Buy stamps for invitations.		
Bride's mother	Shop for dress. Notify groom's mother of length and color.		
Bride	Shop for going-away outfit.		
Bride and groom	Set a date for apartment hunting and furniture shopping.		
Bride	Select shoes for bridesmaids; have dyed in one dye lot.		
Bride	Select lipstick and nail polish for bridesmaids if you prefer they wear matching shades.		
Groom	Check local requirements for blood tests and		

PERSON RESPONSIBLE	TASK	DUE DATE	DATE COMPLETED
	marriage certificate.		
Bride and groom	Begin planning ceremony:		
	Select music		
	prelude music		
	processional		
	recessional		
	solos		
	congregational hymns		
	instrumental selections		
	music for reception		
	Select; scripture used in ceremony		
	order of service		
	Write or select vows		
	Invite co-officiant (if used)		
	Discuss ceremony plans with pastor		
Bride and groom	Enjoy a relaxing day together!		

TWO MONTHS BEFORE

Bride	Finish addressing invitations.		
Bride	Check to see that		

Person Responsible	Task	Due Date	Date Completed
	wardrobe is in order. Have clothes ready to wear to parties, showers, and so on.		
Bride	Buy gifts for bridesmaids.		
Groom	Buy gifts for best man, ushers.		
Bride	Buy gifts for hospitality committee.		
Bride	Buy wedding memory book/guest book.		
Groom	Reserve hotel rooms or make arrangements with relatives and friends to care for out-of-town guests.		
Bride	If you plan to display your gifts, arrange to rent tables and cloths if necessary.		
Bride	Plan bridesmaids' luncheon, if desired.		
Groom	Plan bachelor party, if desired.		
Bride	Change name and address on magazine subscriptions.		
Bride and groom	Begin collecting boxes for move.		
Bride	Begin writing		

PERSON RESPONSIBLE	TASK	DUE DATE	DATE COMPLETED
	thank-you notes for shower gifts received.		
ONE MONTH BEFORE			
Bride	Mail invitations.		
Bride	Make a master list of guests' names if reply cards are used.		
Bride	Buy your wedding gift for the groom.		
Groom	Buy your wedding gift for the bride.		
Bride	Arrange for final fitting of wedding gown. (Be sure to take shoes and lingerie to be worn with it.)		
Bride	Have a black-and-white glossy (for newspaper) and formal portrait taken, if desired.		
Bride	Check your calendar to be sure you have time planned to relax.		
Bride and groom	Select and order covers for bulletins.		
Bride and groom	Make appointments for blood tests.		

PERSON RESPONSIBLE	TASK	DUE DATE	DATE COMPLETED
Bride	Set up gift display.		
Bride	Write the announcement for your newspaper and send it with a black-and-white glossy photo.		
Bride and groom	Make a packing list for your honeymoon. Buy any necessary items.		
Bride and groom	Make out wills.		
Bride and groom	Change name of beneficiary on all insurance policies.		
Bride	Obtain a floater insurance policy to cover wedding gift.		
Bride and groom	As much as possible, pack and move your possessions into your new home.		
Bride	Change name on all credit cards.		.
Bride and groom	Open joint checking and savings accounts.		
Bride	Make hair appointment for several days before the wedding.		
Groom	Make appointment		

Person Responsible	Task	Due Date	Date Completed
	for haircut a week or two before the wedding.		
Groom	Arrange for a friend to stay in the room where gifts are displayed on the wedding day.		
Bride	If it seems necessary, hire a guard to watch the gifts the day before and day of the wedding.		
Bride	If you're a strong traditionalist, do you have:		
	something old		
	something new		
	something borrowed		
	something blue		

THREE WEEKS BEFORE

Person Responsible	Task	Due Date	Date Completed
Bride	Address and stamp announcements to be mailed after the wedding. Give these to a responsible friend.		
Bride	Check with		

PERSON RESPONSIBLE	TASK	DUE DATE	DATE COMPLETED
	bridesmaids to be sure dresses are fitted and shoes ready.		
Groom	Order tuxedos for groom, best man, ushers, fathers.		
Bride and groom	✓ Arrange transportation for any out-of-town guests without cars.		
Bride	Meet with florist to order flowers for:		
	sanctuary		
	bride's bouquet		
	bridesmaids' bouquets		
	flower girl's basket		
	corsages for: mothers, guest-book attendant, soloists, servers at reception		
	boutonnieres for groom, best man, ushers, fathers		
	flowers for reception tables		
Bride	Order wedding cake.		
Bride	Check final details with caterer.		
Bride	Check any details with photographer.		

Person Responsible	Task	Due Date	Date Completed
Bride and groom	Get marriage license. (Be sure to take birth certificate; order a duplicate.)		
Bride	Engage policeman or attendant to direct parking if needed.		
Bride	Engage nursery keepers if needed.		
Bride	Send reserved-pew cards or tell special guests and family members where they are to sit.		
Bride and groom	Plan wording of bulletin. Double-check spelling of all names. Take to typesetter.		
Bride	Make a list of reserved seating to give to ushers, in case guests forget their cards.		
Bride	Make confetti or bags of rice to be tossed as you are going away.		
Bride and groom	Plan your rehearsal dinner in detail: seating plan place cards		

PERSON RESPONSIBLE	TASK	DUE DATE	DATE COMPLETED
	confirm reservation and menu		
	master of ceremonies (usually chosen by the groom)		
	decide who will open in prayer; who will make introductions; when and how gifts will be given to attendants		
	arrange transportation		
Bride	Send invitations to all who will be attending rehearsal. Include maps if necessary.		

TWO WEEKS BEFORE

Bride and groom	Wrap gifts for attendants.		
Bride and groom	Notify all attendants of schedule.		
Groom	Plan to have your get-away car hidden,		

Person Responsible	Task	Due Date	Date Completed
	unless you want tin cans and streamers.		
Bride	Make maps for out-of-town guests.		
Bride	Count the number of guests who have accepted the reception invitation and notify the caterer.		
Bride	Arrange a place for your bridesmaids and yourself to dress before the wedding.		
Bride or groom	Arrange for someone to take any gifts received at the wedding to your home.		
Bride and groom	Meet with the pastor to arrange all details of the rehearsal. Plan the time schedule, which aisles will be used (if the church has no center aisle), where members of the wedding party will stand. Review the service in detail with him.		
Groom	Have car checked for trip.		

PERSON RESPONSIBLE	TASK	DUE DATE	DATE COMPLETED
ONE WEEK BEFORE			
Groom	Get film for camera.		
Bride	While you are still thinking clearly, recheck your packing list for the honeymoon.		
Bride	List everything you'll need for a going-away handbag.		
Bride	List everything that your mother or best friend should return to your home after the wedding.		
Bride	Plan a supply of sandwiches and snacks for the wedding party and any others who will be in your home. Buy groceries.		
Bride	If you are going early to the church for photographs, plan a supply of sandwiches, cheese, crackers, or fruit to take along for		

PERSON RESPONSIBLE	TASK	DUE DATE	DATE COMPLETED
	snacks. Include napkins and wet-wipe tissues.		
Bride	Make an emergency kit—scissors, nail file, spot remover, safety pins, bobby pins, facial tissues, extra pantyhose—to take to the church. Also take an iron for last-minute pressing.		
Bride	Make wedding-day schedule for yourself and tape it to your mirror. Allow plenty of extra time so that even if Great-aunt Agatha calls, you won't be rushed.		
Bride	Arrange for someone to care for pets on the wedding day. They become excited when you're excited. And if Fido escapes, you'll be upset.		
Bride	Press your wedding dress and going-away dress.		
Bride	Make a time schedule		

Person Responsible	Task	Due Date	Date Completed
	for everyone involved in the wedding and either mail or distribute at the rehearsal.		
Bride	Make a list of things to be taken to the rehearsal:		
	gifts for attendants		
	time charts		
	wedding-service bulletins		
	matches for lighting candles		
	marriage license to be given to minister		
Groom	Pick up bulletins.		
Groom	Get traveler's checks.		
Groom	Put minister's fee in envelope and give it to the best man.		
Groom	Confirm hotel reservation for honeymoon night.		
Bride	Talk with head usher about any special seating arrangements.		
Bride	Review the guest list to help you remember names.		

PERSON RESPONSIBLE	TASK	DUE DATE	DATE COMPLETED
Bride and groom	Pack honeymoon luggage in the car the night before the wedding. Be sure gas tank is filled.		

THE WEDDING DAY

Bride	This is it! Sleep late, if you possibly can. Be sure to eat breakfast. Bathe slowly. And use a light touch with your makeup.		
Bride and groom	You have finished all the work. Now you can enjoy the most glorious day of your lives. Savor each moment. Happy wedding!		

AFTER THE WEDDING

Bride	Mail the announcements the day after the wedding (unless you've given		

PERSON RESPONSIBLE	TASK	DUE DATE	DATE COMPLETED
	this duty to a parent or friend).		
Bride	Have the wedding gown professionally cleaned and preserved in an air-tight box.		
Bride and groom	Finish those thank-you notes!		
Bride	After returning from the honeymoon change your name on Social Security card and driver's license. You will need your marriage certificate for this.		

Names and Numbers

Nothing can frazzle your nerves like a misplaced number. List all essential names, addresses, and telephone numbers here for ready reference.

Minister

Groom's parents

Wedding consultant

Caterer

Photographer (for wedding)

Photographer (portrait)

Florist

Organist

Soloist

Other musicians

Department stores where registered

Gynecologist
Bridesmaids

Restaurant for rehearsal
Store where gown is
  purchased
Ushers   Bakery
                                Beautician
                                Tuxedo rental
                                Others

Hospitality committee

4
Budgeting Your Wedding

There's dad, looking forlorn, his empty pockets hanging out. Wedding photographers include it as stock humor. But for many families, the wedding expense is no laughing matter.

The joy of your wedding day is determined not by the amount of money spent, but by the commitment you make. You want a happy, memorable day shared with your families and special friends. You can achieve this without lavish expense. Thoughtful planning will make your wedding outstanding without putting a financial strain on you or your family.

Although it might not sound romantic, budgeting your wedding is wise. Decide in advance how much money you have to spend, then plan your expenditures to fit your budget. If you don't, you could end up like one bride who spent freely on flowers and frills. But because she failed to plan ahead, her money ran out, leaving no option but to buy the groom's ring at a discount store. Or you may overspend on your wedding, leaving little with which to furnish your first home.

If your budget is limited—and most are—decide what means the most to you. That's where you spend your money, compromising or eliminating less important items. Limiting your spending brings an advantage. As the two of you learn to work with your wedding budget, you are forming good patterns of money management. By learning to reconcile your dreams with your cash, you will develop a realistic approach that can save you arguments and heartaches in your marriage.

Challenge yourselves to plan a worshipful service without lavish expense. You'll probably discover that less is more. Simplicity has charm. By concentrating on the service itself and the vows you exchange, you will center attention on lasting values. Your guests, also, will remember the spirit of worship rather than the show.

Throughout this book, you will find suggestions for trimming your budget. By carefully planning the total effect, you can have a wedding you will enjoy at a price you can afford.

Compare Costs

The budget work sheets provide space for estimating costs. The best way to do this is to ask another recent bride, if you know her well, to list her expenses. This will give you ball-park figures. Circle the set expenses, such as the marriage license and minister's fee. Then cross out all items which you do not wish to include. Project amounts to spend for each remaining item until your expenses are *less* than your actual budget. This gives you leeway for those surprise expenses that are bound to arise.

When I first became engaged, I used this procedure. I asked two brides, whose weddings had seemed in my budget range, to list their expenses. Each was shocked to see the total. I was even more shocked! Could we afford the church wedding we wanted? If we spent our money freely on the wedding, we would fulfill our dreams for a day. But we would have nothing left to enjoy on our honeymoon. Nor would we have money for decorating our first home.

As we discussed our values together, we agreed that we wanted a worshipful church ceremony to which we could invite all our friends. Since neither of us wanted to limit our guest list, we chose to limit the food served at the reception. We also wanted to save some funds for our honeymoon and first home. With that in mind, we began trimming our budget. When our wedding day arrived, we were both happy with the results.

We found that the things that seemed so important before the wedding faded in significance afterward. We remembered most of the vows we exchanged, the relationship we began, and the special friends who surrounded us with their love.

Traditional Wedding Expenses

Traditionally almost all of the wedding expenses have gone to the bride's family. The bride pays for the groom's ring, his wedding gift, gifts for her attendants, personal stationery, and her medical examination. The groom pays for the marriage license, his medical examination, the engagement and wedding rings for the bride, the bride's bouquet, boutonnieres for the men and corsages for both mothers, gifts for the men in the wedding party, wedding gift for the bride, his wedding attire, fee for the clergyman, and the honeymoon.

The bride's parents pay for everything else.

Although this breakdown is traditional, it is not law. Today the groom's family may volunteer to help with some of the expenses, such as the reception. Or if both bride and groom are working, they may pay for the wedding, working out the expenses between them. Select the arrangement that best suits your circumstances.

Budget Work Sheet

	Estimated Cost	Actual Cost
Engagement Party		
Invitations		
Postage		
Food/Caterer		
Music		
Flowers and decorations		
Tips to waiters		
Stationery		
Invitations		
Announcements		
Reply cards		
At-home cards		
Thank-you notes		
Postage for all of the above		
Informal notes		
Monogrammed stationery		
Clothing		
Wedding dress		
Cleaning and preserving		
Headpiece and veil		
Shoes		
Slip		

	Estimated Cost	Actual Cost
Jewelry		
Special clothes for showers, rehearsal dinner, and so on		
Going-away outfit		
Clothes for honeymoon		
Groom's tuxedo or suit		
MEDICAL EXPENSES		
Gynecological examination		
Birth control		
Blood tests		
GIFTS		
Engagement ring		
Bride's wedding ring		
Groom's wedding ring		
Bride's wedding gift		
Groom's wedding gift		
Ushers' gifts		
Bridesmaids' gifts		
Gifts for friends serving at reception		
BRIDESMAIDS' LUNCHEON		
Food/catering		
Tips for waiters		

	Estimated Cost	Actual Cost
Flowers or centerpiece		
Corsages		
Bachelor Party		
Food/catering		
Tips for waiters		
Photographs		
Black-and-white glossy		
Formal portrait		
Official photographs taken during wedding and reception		
Informal/candids taken by friends		
Duplicates to give to friends, relatives		
Rehearsal Dinner		
Food/catering		
Tips for waiters		
Invitations		
Postage		
Flowers and/or centerpiece		

	ESTIMATED COST	ACTUAL COST
MUSIC		
Organist's fee		
Fee or gift for soloist		
Other musicians		
Purchased sheet music		
FLORIST		
Flowers for sanctuary		
Bride's bouquet		
Bridesmaids' bouquets		
Flower girl's basket		
Ring bearer's pillow		
Corsages for mothers and grandmothers		
Corsages for friend attending guest book		
Boutonnieres for: groom best man ushers fathers		
Flowers for reception: cake table centerpieces for buffet centerpiece for head table corsages for friends who serve		

	Estimated Cost	Actual Cost
WEDDING		
Rental of church		
Minister's fee		
Pew ribbons		
Aisle runner		
Candles		
Rental of candelabra		
Rental of kneeler		
Fee for custodian		
Guest book and pen		
Bulletins:		
cover		
typesetting		
Nursery attendants		
Gratuity for traffic officer, parking attendants		
RECEPTION		
Rental of site		
Rental of special serving pieces		
punch bowl		
coffee service		
tables		
table skirts		
plates, cups, silverware		
Music		

Catering service(or food costs)
   punch ingredients

	ESTIMATED COST	ACTUAL COST
coffee, cream, sugar other food		
Wedding cake		
Personalized napkins		
Keepsake knife for cutting cake		
Keepsake plate		
Keepsake wedding cup		
Rose petals, rice, or confetti		
Tips for doorman, waiters		
Table favors		
Gratuity for traffic officer		
FEES		
Marriage license		
Bridal consultant		
OTHER		
Additional insurance to cover wedding gifts		
Security guard to protect gifts		
Rental of tables, cloths for displaying gifts		
Tape of wedding ceremony		
Transportation for guests		
POST-WEDDING EXPENSES		
Honeymoon		
Moving		

5
Determining the Guest List

Many of your budget decisions depend upon the number of guests invited. Do you prefer an intimate gathering? Or do you want all your friends and church congregation to celebrate? Do you plan to serve punch and cake? A light buffet? A meal? The more food you serve, the more you will need to limit your guest list.

The bride's family traditionally determines the size of the guest list, allowing the groom's family to invite half the guests. However, it seldom works out exactly. Much depends upon where the two families live. If the bride and groom are paying for their wedding, then they determine the number of guests to invite.

Begin making your guest list as soon as possible. Call or write the groom's mother, telling her of your plans. Let her know how many guests she may include on her list, and a date by which you need all names and addresses. If you use a file index, send her a sample card. If your fiancé's family is some distance away, you might ask how many acceptances you are likely to get.

Begin writing your guest list by categories. Start with the musts: brothers and sisters (with their wives and husbands) of both bride and groom, members of your wedding party with their spouses or intendeds, and the minister and his wife.

Now continue your list with relatives; friends of the family; neighbors; friends from school, church, business, and so on. Allow yourself some time and keep a notebook handy in your purse. You'll probably think of names at odd times.

A Good Investment in Time

When your list is complete, assemble your equipment to make a card index. This takes a surprising amount of time, but it's one of the best investments you can make. This card file will speed the process of addressing invitations, will aid in recording gifts, and will be used again when you write your thank-you notes. Afterward, it becomes a permanent address file.

You'll need a file box or Rolodex, index cards, and alphabetical dividers. On each card write or type the name of each guest, and children, and complete address. If you are not inviting all the guests to the reception, use two colors of cards to distinguish which should get reception invitations or put an *R* in the corner of the card. Sample:

> Mr. and Mrs. Peter Renfer
> 1305 South Washington Avenue
> Canton, Michigan 48187

Alphabetize by last names to spot duplicates quickly.

If you are requesting responses to your reception, make a master alphabetical list of all guests invited. Tape this to the back of a door. As replies come in, cross out those who decline, and mark the number attending beside those who accept. When it is time to give the total to your caterer, it will be easy to tally. Although this system takes a bit longer in the beginning than marking acceptances on your index file, it will save you time when you need it most.

6
Inviting Your Guests

Selecting the Invitations

A small wedding does not require engraved invitations. Instead, the mother of the bride (or the bride) may write short notes or telephone relatives and friends who are invited.

For a larger wedding, select invitations from a stationer, either at a stationery store or at a department store. Traditional invitations are engraved in black ink on the first page of a double sheet. The paper is white, ivory, or ecru. However, photoengraving is now available that looks similar to engraving—even with raised letters—and at a third the cost. When used on plain white, ivory, or ecru paper, these invitations maintain formal dignity and simplicity.

Invitations are also available in a wide range of colors, designs, and folds. Some can include a picture of the couple. Others have a message or Scripture verse on the outside, with the invitation inside the card. Although these depart from tradition, they may express your individuality.

Budget trimmer: If formal invitations are not important to you, you might have your invitations printed. One bride designed invitations to be printed on eight-and-one-half-by-eleven sheets. She folded and addressed these on the outside, eliminating envelopes altogether. Informal? Yes, but her guests got the message, and she held down her wedding costs.

When ordering invitations, allow at least four to six weeks for delivery. If possible, allow extra time in case of mistake by the engraver or loss by the postal service.

One printer advises ordering at least twenty-five more invitations than you think you'll possibly need. Almost every bride calls later to order extras, he says, and by then it's too late.

Order invitations and all stationery supplies at the same time. You'll need thank-you notes for shower and wedding gifts, and you might want informal notes with your married names. If you will be using monogrammed note paper or engraved calling cards, order these as well.

Wording Your Invitations

Formal wording of the invitation follows this form:

Mr. and Mrs. Allan Kingsley
request the honour of your presence
at the marriage of their daughter
Sarah Anne
to
Mr. George David Johnson
on Saturday, the tenth of June
One thousand nine hundred and eighty-five
at two o'clock
Emmanuel Baptist Church
1449 Main Street
Chicago

Mention of the year is optional. If the church is well-known, the street address may be omitted. The time of the ceremony, usually on the hour or on the half hour, is written

out. If it is to be on the half hour the wording reads *at half
after two* or *at half past two*. The abbreviations *Mr., Mrs.,
Dr.,* or *Jr.* may be used, but all other words are written out.
If the bride's mother is divorced, the invitation reads:

Mrs. Smith Kingsley
[the mother's maiden name plus her divorced
husband's name]
requests the honour of your presence
at the marriage of her daughter
Sarah Anne

If the bride's mother, either widowed or divorced, has
remarried, the invitation reads:

Mr. and Mrs. Daniel Thompson
request the honour of your presence
at the marriage of Mrs. Thompson's daughter
Sarah Anne Kingsley

Or she may issue the invitations in her name alone:

Mrs. Daniel Thompson
requests the honour of your presence
at the marriage of her daughter
Sarah Anne Kingsley

For a double wedding, in which the brides are sisters, the
invitation reads:

Mr. and Mrs. Allan Kingsley
request the honour of your presence
at the marriage of their daughters
Sarah Anne
to
Mr. George David Johnson

and
Janet Marie
to
Mr. Timothy Dale Carpenter

If the brides are just friends, the invitation reads:

Mr. and Mrs. Allan Kingsley
and
Mr. and Mrs. James Rollins
request the honour of your presence
at the marriage of their daughters
Sarah Anne Kingsley
to
Mr. George David Johnson
and
Linda Lee Rollins
to
Mr. Lance Livingston

Sometimes the parents of the bride and groom issue the invitation jointly. If so, the invitation reads:

Mr. and Mrs. Allan Kingsley
and
Mr. and Mrs. John Johnson
request the honour of your presence
at the marriage of their children
Sarah Anne
to
Mr. George David Johnson
and
Janet Marie
to
Mr. Timothy Dale Carpenter

If a young bride has no close relatives or if an older bride wishes to issue her own invitation, it would read:

The honour of your presence
is requested at the marriage of
Miss Deborah Lynn Taylor
to
Mr. John Calvin Moore

If the bride and groom are giving their wedding together, the invitation might read:

Miss Susan Jane Warrington
and
Mr. Richard Martin Myers
together with their parents [optional]
request the honour of your presence

Nontraditional Invitations

Today's brides often forego the formal wording to make their invitations more personal or to include a witness to their faith in Christ. If you wish to depart from tradition, be sure to follow the general format for time and place of the ceremony. And follow the rules regarding abbreviations. Check with your stationer to be sure your wording will fit the invitations you select. Here are some samples of nontraditional invitations.

With thanksgiving to God
who has established marriage and has prepared
Janice Joy Bohrer
and
Mark Hale Pruitt
to be united in marriage

we,
Mr. and Mrs. Richard Bohrer
and
Mr. and Mrs. Rex C. Pruitt
invite you to worship with us, witness their vows,
and share in their love for one another
on Saturday, the thirtieth of June,
Nineteen hundred and seventy-nine,
at two o'clock in the afternoon
Lake Baptist Church
Lake Oswego, Oregon

With Christian joy
Daisy Kay Oliver
and
Thomas Martin Lewis
together with their parents
invite you to worship and celebrate
as they unite their lives in holy matrimony
on Saturday the seventeenth of May
Nineteen hundred and eighty
at half past two
Cuyler Covenant Church
Byron and Marshfield
Chicago

God has ordained that one man and one woman
shall be joined together
in love and companionship . . .
Mr. and Mrs. Reuben Hanson
invite you to share in their joy
as their daughter
Kathryn Ruth
and
Glen Joseph Wagner

become united in Christ
on Saturday, the twenty-fourth of September
Nineteen hundred and seventy-seven
at one o'clock in the afternoon
Cuyler Covenant Church
Chicago
If you are unable to attend, we
ask your presence in thought in prayer

Invitation Enclosures

Pew cards: Today it is relatively rare for an invitation to include a pew card. However, if such a card is used, it is handwritten in black ink and reads:

Groom's or [Bride's] Reserved Section
Mr. and Mrs. Harrison Collins

Reception cards: If everyone invited to the wedding is also invited to the reception, a line may be included at the bottom of the invitation:

And afterward at the reception
[Give location, if not at the church]

Or the minister may issue the invitation to the reception immediately following the recessional and before guests are dismissed.

When all those attending the wedding are not invited to the reception, a reception card of the same stock as the invitation is included. It reads:

Mr. and Mrs. Allan Kingsley
request the pleasure of your company
at the wedding dinner

following the ceremony
at
Elliot's Pine Log
7578 North Lincoln
Chicago
R.S.V.P.

Response cards: An R.S.V.P. on the reception card indicates that the recipient is to respond with a formal reply. Thus, no printed response card is necessary. Such cards, however, are available and convenient both to the guest and to the bride. If these cards are used, their envelopes must be stamped by the bride.

At-home cards: These are often included in announcements, and less frequently in invitations. If they are included with the invitation, they must not bear the name of the couple, because they are not yet married. These cards are smaller than the reception card, and should be of the same stock and type style as the invitation or announcement. Abbreviations are permitted.

If the at-home card goes out with the announcement, it reads:

Mr. and Mrs. Harold Henderson
after the fifth of June
1117 South Dryden
St. Louis, MO 63137

If it goes out with the invitation, it reads:

Will be at home
after the fifth of June
1117 South Dryden
St. Louis, MO 63137

Maps: If many of your guests will need directions to either the church or the reception, include a small map with your invitation.

Addressing the Invitation

The addressing of wedding invitations and announcements is one of the most time-consuming tasks you'll have, so allow plenty of time. Although the rules seem rigid, they are simple. So learn them, then address your invitations with confidence.

These must be handwritten in black ink. The only abbreviations permitted are *Dr., Mr., Mrs.,* and *Jr.* or the initial of a name if you don't know it in full. Everything else, including the street name and the state, must be written in full. Use no figures except for the house number and zip code. *Twenty-seventh Street* must be written out.

The correct form for the outer envelope is:

> Mr. and Mrs. James David Millet
> 6508 Ashley Lane
> Dallas, Texas 75214

Never write *and family* on the outer envelope. Instead, include this information on the inner envelope:

> Mr. and Mrs. Millet
> [no first name]
> Christine and Daniel
> [if the children are minors]

If an adult son or daughter or other man or woman is in the household, he or she should receive a separate invitation:

Miss Cara Millet
6508 Ashley Lane
Dallas, Texas 75214

The inside envelope reads:

Miss Millet

For two adult sisters write: *Misses Susan and Melinda Millet* on the outer envelope and *Misses Millet* on the inner envelope.

For two grown sons, write: *Messrs. David and John Millet* on the outer envelope and *Messrs. Millet* inside.

For a widow, write: *Mrs. Robert Martin* (never *Mrs. Alice Martin*) and *Mrs. Martin* inside.

For a divorcée, use *Mrs. Thompson Martin* (her maiden name, if you know it, combined with her former husband's name) and *Mrs. Martin inside.*

It is improper to write *no children* on invitations. If children are not invited, do not include their names on the inner envelope.

At my wedding I wanted my friends to bring their children, but I did not want cries disturbing the service. I included all children's names on the invitations, then wrote *nursery provided* if the children were age four or younger. Parents seemed to appreciate this.

Return addresses: For strictly formal invitations, return addresses must be embossed (which is very expensive) on the flap or handwritten either in the upper left-hand corner of the envelope or on the flap. You may choose to ignore the formal rules and have a return address printed on the flap. For a large wedding, this can save hours.

Mailing: Folded invitations are inserted in the inner (ungummed) envelope with the folded edge down. The engraved side should face the back of the envelope. The tissue is placed over the engraving. The inner envelope is then placed in the outer envelope so the writing faces the back of the outer envelope.

Always send invitations and announcements sealed, first-class mail. Place the stamps carefully, and never use a postal meter. Invitations are mailed four weeks before the wedding. Announcements are mailed immediately after the wedding.

Announcements: These are sent only to those not invited to the wedding. They read:

Mr. and Mrs. Allan Kingsley
have the honour of announcing
the marriage of their daughter
Sarah Anne
to
Mr. George David Johnson
on Saturday, the tenth of June
Nineteen hundred and eighty-five
Emmanuel Baptist Church
Chicago

7
Your Attendants

The very simplest wedding must have one bridesmaid and one groomsman to stand as witnesses. You may also have more bridesmaids and ushers, a junior bridesmaid, flower girl, and ring bearer. Be sure that child attendants are old enough to take the pressure of public performance. And be sure you're willing for them to steal the show!

Before inviting your friends to be attendants, be thoughtful. Will participating in your wedding mean travel expenses? Will the wedding outfit strain his or her budget? Will the added bouquets and gifts strain your budget? And how many attendants will comfortably fit at the front of the church or other wedding site?

The Bride's Attendants

Select as many of your sisters and best friends as seem appropriate without turning the wedding into a parade. Invite other close friends to participate by attending to your guest book, assisting with gifts, and serving at your reception.

Bridesmaids' duties: Bridesmaids are strictly decorative. But the maid or matron of honor has a specific role. She walks down the aisle just before the bride (unless a flower girl is used). She keeps the groom's ring until the bride gives it to him. And she holds the bride's bouquet during the ceremony. As the recessional begins, she straightens the bride's veil and train and then follows the bride and groom down the aisle. She will also assist the bride in any way she can during preparations for the wedding.

Bridesmaids' dresses: Try to select dresses that will harmonize with your dress both in style and fabric and that can be worn after the wedding. A dress that can be cut to street length will be appreciated. Be thoughtful also in selecting a style and color flattering to each girl.

The dresses may be chosen at a bridal salon or bridal section of a department store. Here matching dresses can be ordered in any size, with professional alterations made for an additional fee. Bridesmaids will need to make appointments for fittings after you have selected the dresses.

Or you can select a pattern and fabric for them to sew. Be certain first that each girl has the time and ability, or has a dressmaker available. Because patterns fit individuals differently, and because seamstresses can vary in their technique, the dresses may not be exactly uniform. But the girls may appreciate the money saved.

You might be able to find suitable dresses in the evening-wear section of a department store. If you can find matching dresses in the right sizes, they will cost about half the amount of those ordered in a bridal salon.

Traditionally bridesmaids have worn shoes dyed to match their dresses. More and more modern brides, however, allow their attendants to wear white or neutral shoes that can be worn after the wedding.

The Groom's Attendants

The groom chooses his ushers and best man. The best man can be a brother, close friend, or even his father. Although he should have as many attendants as the bride has bridesmaids, he can allow his ushers to double as groomsmen, or he can select separate ushers (one per every fifty guests).

Duties of the best man: Like the maid/matron of honor, the best man has specific duties. He is advisor, messenger, and general assistant to the groom. Traditionally, he rouses the groom on the morning of the wedding. He helps the groom dress on that day, making sure his tie is straight and boutonniere is in place.

The best man makes sure the groom has the marriage license, and keeps the bride's wedding ring until time to give it during the ceremony. He gives the minister his fee in an envelope before the ceremony. And he, along with the maid/matron of honor, is one of the witnesses who signs the marriage certificate.

Duties of ushers: The groom's ushers also have specified duties. They must arrive at the church an hour before the ceremony, where they will receive their boutonnieres. They will seat all guests. If some pews have been reserved, the ushers should have a list of guests to be seated in the re-served section. If the bride and groom so instruct, ushers may ask guests "friend of bride?" or "friend of groom?" so they may be correctly seated—on the left side of the church for the bride, and on the right for the groom. Or ushers may balance the seating.

Regardless of the number of guests arriving, ushers should be gracious and unhurried and must escort each guest or group of guests. If several guests arrive in a group, the usher offers his right arm to the eldest lady, and the others follow. If two women arrive together, he offers his arm to the elder, leaving the younger to wait his return or to be escorted by another usher. If a woman arrives with her husband or es-cort, the usher takes her to her seat while the man follows a few steps behind. A male guest entering alone is seated by the usher, although he does not offer his arm unless the man is very aged. Children follow as their parents are ushered down the aisle.

Five minutes before the beginning of the processional, the groom's mother is ushered to her seat (the first pew on the right). If her husband is with her, he follows her down the aisle. Other family members may also be seated in that pew.

The head usher escorts the bride's mother to her seat (the first pew on the left). Her entrance signals that the processional is ready to begin. After the bride's mother is seated, no one else is to be seated by an usher. Late-arriving guests must either wait outside or quickly seat themselves at the back of the church.

After the bride's mother is seated, two ushers roll out the aisle runner, if one is used, then take their places for the processional. After the recessional two ushers escort the mothers of the bride and groom. They then return to dismiss the guests by pews.

Men's wedding attire: Usually the groom, his best man, the ushers, and the father of the bride all rent tuxedos. The groom selects a style and color that will harmonize with the bride's and bridesmaids' gowns. Each man in the wedding party must then go to be fitted and to place his order. Each pays for his own tuxedo rental.

Budget Trimmer: The groom may choose to buy a suit instead. If he is having only a best man, they can arrange to wear suits of similar or complementary colors. Ushers then would wear dark suits.

Gifts for Attendants

The bride and groom give each of their attendants a gift to express their thanks. These may be given either at the bridesmaids' luncheon and bachelor party, if such are held, or at the rehearsal dinner. Traditionally, brides give gold or silver jewelry, engraved with the wedding date. Grooms give cuff links, pen and pencil sets, paperweights, or letter openers.

Modern trends, however, allow the couple to select any gift they think their attendants would enjoy. These gifts could be other jewelry articles, small totable umbrellas, plants, tickets to a concert or sports event, books, or whatever else you think would please your attendants.

Ask Others to Participate

Those who love you most will want to participate in the joy of your wedding. As you make your plans, think of ways to include others. Although you may be hesitant to ask for assistance, you will find that most people feel honored that you think enough of them to want their help. The more you involve others, the more your community of friends will surround you with the love and support you need.

Think about the abilities of the people you know. Can some sing? Play instruments? Make artistic banners? Print invitations or programs? Invite them to make their contributions.

Do you know someone who could help with decorating the church or reception site? A cake baker? An organizer to run the reception? Let them share the blessing by giving their abilities. You could invite friends to bring a special dish for the rehearsal buffet or your wedding reception.

Perhaps you could ask close friends or an uncle and aunt to be host and hostess. Assign specific duties to each, such as distributing flowers to the wedding party, seeing that bridesmaids and ushers enter at the correct time, receiving gifts, greeting guests, and giving directions at the reception.

Think of ways for people to participate in your ceremony. Rather than have your guests be spectators at a pageant, allow them to be worshipers together by singing hymns and reading Scripture. If you think people will feel comfortable, allow a time in the ceremony for guests to offer spontaneous prayers or expressions of love. At your reception have a microphone available and invite guests to say something personal about their relationship with you.

During the ceremony, allow guests to ring bells or light candles. Give each a flower, or invite friends to bring a flower to add to a growing bouquet. For an outdoor wedding, you could have a circle of white fabric where the bride, groom, and minister will stand. Guests could place their flowers around the perimeter to form a wreath.

By involving the larger community of people, you say that you cannot live marriage alone. You need the love and prayers of others.

Attendants' Checklist

ATTENDANT	ATTIRE	DATE FITTED	GIFT
Maid/Matron of Honor			
Bridesmaids			
Junior Bridesmaid			
Flower Girl			
Ring Bearer			
Best Man			
Ushers			

8
Your Wedding Gown

Feeling a tug at my wedding gown, I looked just in time to see my friend's three-year-old daughter blush, then run. Soon she mustered the courage to return, stretching her arms to be lifted into my lap. Usually a chatterbox, she sat in awe, then dusted my cheek with a soft kiss.

Dreams of a long, white gown begin early.

Now it's your turn to translate that dream into reality. No doubt you've already paged through bridal magazines, trying to determine your taste. Taste, budget, and sentimental value will help guide your decision.

Think carefully about the sentimental value of the dress. Will you want to keep it to wear on anniversaries or show your children? Will you have a place to store it? Or will you be satisfied to preserve your dress with pictures?

Before you begin shopping, consider some of the options.

Buy a gown at a bridal salon: These specialty shops have the largest selection of gowns in a wide range of prices. The bridal salon also has a selection of veils, accessories, bridesmaids' dresses, and dresses for mothers. Everything can be conveniently arranged with one shopping trip.

Before entering, determine what you can spend. Ask the salesperson to show only gowns in that range. Gowns purchased in these stores must be specially ordered and will take up to two months for delivery.

Although gowns bought in salons are generally expensive,

these stores have substantial off-season and sample sales. If you have plenty of time, ask when the next sale is scheduled.

Some bridal salons exert heavy sales pressure. Be prepared to deal tactfully but firmly with any salesperson who tries to force you to place an order immediately. You are in charge and have every right to wait or shop elsewhere before deciding. Most of these stores also want you to give your name, telephone number, and place and time of wedding. This information is then sold to florists, caterers, photographers, and others in the wedding industry. If you do not wish to receive telephone solicitations (usually at dinner time), do not give this information.

Buy at a department store: Most large stores have bridal departments, although they may not have as large a selection as a bridal salon. You'll need an appointment, and the gowns must be ordered with two-month wait for delivery. Prices are similar to a bridal salon.

Rent a gown: Check your Yellow Pages to see whether your city has a rental service for bridal gowns. These carry a variety of styles and sizes which can be altered. All gowns are cleaned after each use, so they look fresh. You won't have your gown to save, of course, but neither will you have the expense of cleaning and storing it.

Use an heirloom: Does your mother or grandmother still have her wedding dress, her veil? If they are your taste and size, wear them with pride.

Sew your gown: Your groom will think he's marrying a genius. If you have moderate sewing skills, this project isn't as difficult as it might seem. Or you might hire a seamstress. Allow plenty of time. First, make a model at least of the bodice in muslin or an old sheet. Then you can cut into the good fabric confident that it will fit.

Sewing gives you exactly what you want at a lower cost. You'll enjoy your workmanship—and the gleam in your groom's eye. The disadvantage, of course, is the investment in time. And unless you test the pattern first, it might not look or fit as you envisioned.

Borrow your dress: A good friend (married more than a year) about your size might be delighted to have you wear her dress. She'll feel honored that you appreciate her taste and glad that her dress can get further use. You'll enjoy the convenience and the savings. Be sure to have the dress professionally cleaned and preserved before returning it.

Budget trimmer: Need to purchase a gown, but the prices seem high? Look carefully at the bridesmaids' gowns. These cost considerably less, and can be ordered in white. When adorned with a veil, it will look thoroughly official.

Or you may be able to find a suitable dress hidden among the prom dresses in the junior department. Many times they carry lacy white or off-white dresses that look like wedding gowns. This dress won't have a train, of course. But when you add a veil and bouquet, the effect is just as pretty—and the savings astronomical!

Also watch the classified section of the newspaper. You may find someone selling a gown in your size and taste. Don't depend on this, but it never hurts to look.

Accessories

After selecting your wedding gown, you'll want a fingertip or full-length veil or a garland of flowers for your hair. Some gowns have veils available with matching lace. Or you may select one that harmonizes with similar lace and color. Even if you plan to make your own, try on several at a bridal shop to see what looks best with your dress and hairstyle.

Budget trimmer: A veil is quite easy to make with patterns available at a fabric store. Some fabric stores have special bridal corners with ready-covered caps or with frames, laces, and beads to design your own. These require no sewing—just a bottle of glue.

You'll also need:

Shoes: Traditionally, brides wear white silk or satin. But most modern brides select a plain white leather pump or sandals that can be worn after the wedding. Be sure to buy your shoes before the final fitting of your dress. And whatever you choose for "something new," don't choose shoes! To avoid pinched feet on your wedding day, begin breaking in those shoes, at least around the house.

Lingerie: After selecting your dress you'll know whether you will need a strapless bra (break it in!) or a long slip that adds fullness. Take along any special lingerie for your final fitting.

Jewelry: Strive for simplicity. You might want to wear a strand of pearls or heirloom pin, or no jewelry at all. Earrings should be pearls or small gold posts. Wear no rings other than your engagement ring (worn on your right hand until after the ceremony) and no other diamonds.

Your Trousseau

That quaint word, *trousseau,* means, quite simply, the clothes you take with you into your new life. It is probably unwise to buy an entire new wardrobe. Your tastes and pattern of living could easily change. And though you detest the thought, many brides do gain weight after marriage. Also, because you'll be changing your name and marital identity, and perhaps be making other changes as well, you may welcome something familiar.

Carefully go through the contents of your closet. Were some items not worn in the past year? Discard or give them away. Check to see that everything is clean and that any necessary mending or alterations have been made.

List any items needed to complete your wardrobe, and plan shopping time for these. Also make a detailed list of everything you'll need on your honeymoon and complete your shopping before those final weeks.

Plan your going-away outfit. You may want a new dress or suit that will become the mainstay of your wardrobe. Or you may prefer to leave in a pantsuit or comfortable jeans.

9
Your Most Important Appointment

If you haven't done so already, make an appointment with your gynecologist. He or she will need to see you six to eight weeks before the wedding, but many have a one- or two-month wait for appointments. Your gynecologist will give you a thorough internal exam and answer any questions about sex you may have. He or she can recommend exercises that can make your wedding night more comfortable. He or she will also discuss various methods of birth control and fit you for a diaphram or prescribe birth-control pills, should you choose either of these methods.

Some million-dollar advice: many brides contract an infection of the urethra during the first weeks of marriage, so many in fact that it is called honeymoon urethritis. Although this is not serious, the pain is severe—and very unwelcome on a honeymoon.

According to Dr. Ed Wheat in *Intended for Pleasure,* the urethra is easily bruised, allowing bacteria to grow. The infection then gets pushed into the bladder. Then comes pain, blood in the urine, and severe burning while urinating.

Although this condition is easily treated by a gynecologist, it can be prevented. Drink plenty of water during the day, urinate immediately after intercourse, and wash the outer genitals with soap and water. If even slight discomfort should arise, drink more water and wash each time you urinate.

10
Flowers

Flowers add beauty and festiveness to a wedding. And bouquets hide nervous hands. Depending on your budget, you can choose from several options for floral decorations.

Use a florist: Carefully select a florist with a good reputation for fresh flowers and on-time deliveries. The florist that services your church may be the best choice, since he is already familiar with the sanctuary. Tell him your color scheme, and describe the effect you want to achieve. What bouquets and corsages will you need? What are your favorite flowers? In-season flowers will be more plentiful and thus more economical.

A florist is both the easiest and most expensive option. With only one appointment you can make all decisions. All flowers will be delivered the day of your wedding. Be sure to give the exact time and place for delivery. And keep a receipt.

Ask a capable friend: If you have a friend who can arrange flowers, have her use either flowers from your garden or purchase some from a florist. You might consider silk flowers. Although these are not cheap, they can be found on sale. Because they don't wilt, they can be arranged ahead of time, saving last-minute rush. Your bouquet can become a beautiful centerpiece for your new home. And your bridesmaids' bouquets can be your gift to them.

At the reception: You might want ivy or other greenery

twined on the buffet or cake table, and a centerpiece for the bridal table. (Let bridesmaids' bouquets do double duty.) If you want the florist to provide decorations, be sure to tell him when you place your order.

Budget trimmer: Save on floral bills by decorating with your own house plants. Ferns, palms, or other large plants look lovely, and can be brought back home after the wedding, or given to your bridal party for gifts.

You could carry a small white Bible (cover one with satin) with a few white roses attached. Or carry three roses, with one given to your mother during the processional, and one given to your mother-in-law during the recessional.

Bridesmaids can carry a single rose with long ribbons or small baskets of ivy. For your hospitality committee, make corsages from white bells or sprigs of artificial lily of the valley attached with ribbon to a flocked white leaf. This leaves only boutonnieres and the mothers' corsages to be purchased from a florist.

11
Photographs and Recordings

Pictures and a tape recording of your service will bring back the memories of your special day. Choose your photographer with care, for this is a one-time event. Recommendations from friends are best, for they can tell you not only their satisfaction with the pictures, but also if the photographer was quiet during the ceremony and polite to guests.

Bridal portrait: You may wish to have a formal portrait made at a studio or your home. Look at samples and discuss prices before making your final decision. Many portrait photographers will take formal portraits the day of the wedding. The cost is less than a studio sitting, and a bride always looks her prettiest on her wedding day. However, lighting quality may not be as perfect, and you may feel more rushed.

Do you want black-and-white glossies for a newspaper or duplicates for parents? When you decide, make firm financial arrangements regarding the charges. Get a written statement detailing the costs (with and without an album) and prices of additional prints.

Photos at the wedding and reception: Give your photographer a detailed list of the situations and people you want photographed. Look carefully at his samples. Some photographers specialize in posed shots; others do best at candids. If you do or do not want some of the standard shots (bride's and groom's hands, father showing empty

86

pockets, ushers pointing to their watches, and so on), be sure to say so.

Explain all regulations about photographing inside the church. Because the ceremony is a solemn worship service, it is best not to shoot any pictures at this time except available-light (no flash) photos taken from an obscure spot.

When will your pictures be taken? Old superstition decreed bad luck if the groom saw his bride before the wedding. Many modern couples, however, defy such superstition and enjoy taking pictures before guests arrive. Everyone, and the flowers, look more fresh. And you don't keep guests waiting. Allow two hours before the ceremony to get relaxed, creative pictures. One further advantage is you'll walk the aisle and stand in your positions in your wedding gown, making this a relaxing dress rehearsal.

If you take the pictures after the ceremony, do consider your guests. Perhaps they would enjoy remaining seated to watch the pictures being taken. Or form your receiving line, then allow guests to enjoy punch while they wait.

Would you like to remember the friends who came to your reception? Your wedding photographer can be instructed to take candids. Or an amateur photographer might be glad to do this if you supply the film.

Budget Trimmer: A skilled amateur can take your wedding pictures at a fraction of a professional's cost. Before making this decision, realize that he *is* an amateur and might not get the perfect lighting and exposure expected of a professional. Because he lacks the experience, he might not think of creative poses or might take more time to set up the pictures. On the other hand, his pictures may seem more candid and less staged.

A professional photographer keeps your negatives on file for years, so you can order duplicates in ten years should you lose your originals. An amateur will not be able to provide this service.

If you take this option, be willing to accept the pictures as they are. If poor pictures would risk the loss of a friendship, go with a professional.

12
Wedding Programs

Most worship services include a bulletin to help guide worshipers. You may wish to give guests a printed program to help them follow the ceremony and worship with you. This is especially helpful if you have unusual elements. If you wish the congregation to sing or read Scripture, you will need to have the words printed so all can participate.

You may get wedding bulletins from the same companies that print church-service bulletins. Check with your church office or Christian bookstore.

An artistic friend can design the cover to carry out your wedding theme. You can have the copy typeset or type it yourself. Small printing companies or the firm that prints your church bulletins can print them. Be sure to ask about any specifications, such as margins.

Your wedding program will include the order of events in the ceremony, names and roles of everyone in the wedding party, and title and composer of any music.

You may also include the names and roles of all helpers, such as guest-book attendant, hospitality committee, cake baker, and so on. Include any poems or readings you like, and explain any symbolism that might not be readily understood.

Greeting to Your Guests

This is also a good place for your greeting to guests, thanking them for coming. You might also include a short message expressing your faith in Christ. Here are examples:

Welcome to the celebration of our wedding!

A wedding is covenant and drama. We are acting out the profound realities of love, affection, and commitment to each other. You have played an important part in our lives, and now you participate in the drama of our wedding.

Come, let us exalt His name together!

Thank you for sharing in the joy and worship of this holy occasion. We cherish your friendship and invite your prayers for us as we enter an institution as old as the Garden of Eden, yet so new to us.

Our marriage is our second life-changing event. By far the most important event was when we each acknowledged our sinfulness and received Jesus Christ as our Saviour, recognizing that He paid the penalty for our sin by His death. We now place Jesus Christ as Lord of our lives and Lord of our marriage.

May the Lord bless you, and may you have the joy and peace that come through knowing Christ.

It is especially meaningful to us and to our families that each of you has come to share this joyous occasion with us. We are so thankful for all that God has done in our lives individually to prepare us for our union. The new life He has already given us in Jesus Christ gives us a growing understanding of love and commitment, and is the cornerstone for our life together. Our prayer is that each of you might also personally experience the fullness of God's love in your life through Jesus Christ. We covet your continued prayers for our life together. Thank you for coming.

13
Selecting Music

Music is a powerful way to create the atmosphere you want and to direct corporate worship. Select all music with care and discrimination to accentuate the reverence of the service. Never use music as entertainment or to fill a silent gap.

In selecting your music, look for texts that extol God's love displayed through Christ, the foundation for marriage, His blessing on marriage, and hymns of praise to God. Avoid any songs that promote romanticized or secular ideas about love. These detract from the worship of God.

A wealth of music is available for weddings. A partial list is given at the end of this section. You can also find contemporary Scripture songs at a Christian bookstore or in denominational collections usually available at a music store. Also, ask your vocalist and organist for suggestions. If they participate frequently in weddings, they probably have a collection of suitable music. If your town has a Christian radio station, the music librarian might also make suggestions. Check with your pastor before making any final decisions.

You may want to let your guests join in expressing their praise to God, the Giver of love and marriage. Congregational hymn singing can be effective. You might want to use a congregational hymn for your processional or recessional. Or have a hymn played on the organ for the processional, with the congregation joining in after the wedding party reaches the front of the sanctuary.

You can also use congregational singing for a prayer (such as singing the Lord's Prayer), as a prayer response, or a benediction.

Most use the organ for its majestic tones. Contact your organist soon after the wedding date is set to allow plenty of time to prepare the music you have chosen.

You needn't be limited to the organ. Use a piano also, if you wish. Or have selections played on violin, cello, flute, trumpet, and so on. Musician friends might form a small string ensemble. Consider including your church choir, singing from the balcony.

If you use a vocalist, be sure that the music you select fits with his/her range and ability. You may either first select your music, then find a vocalist who can handle it, or invite a vocalist and choose music accordingly. If you select music that your organist or vocalist do not have, you should purchase this for them.

Times You Will Want Music

You'll want music at several different spots in your wedding. Prelude music provides background as the guests begin their worship. This music can be varied with hymns, classical selections, or contemporary music.

The processional provides music for the wedding party to enter. You may have one selection, or use one for the bridesmaids, and another for the bride.

Music during the service provides a change of pace and directs the flow of worship. Choose two to three selections for the congregation, a vocalist, or an instrumental solo, or use a combination of these. You could have antiphonal singing—alternating a vocal solo with congregational singing. Do not select so many numbers that the wedding becomes a concert. Each selection usually takes about five minutes, and you may tire of standing.

Background music, played during the vows or meditation, is distracting. The words spoken at a wedding are important in their own right, and do not need to be enhanced by music. The music might drown out the words. You might, however, plan a duet of voice and flute for the reading of Scripture.

Secular songs should be reserved for the reception, since this is a social occasion rather than a worship service.

The following is a guide to classical and hymn selections for your wedding. Because contemporary music constantly changes, it is best for you to survey your bookstore.

Music Guide

Classical Preludes

> Bach, J.S.
>> Air on G String
>> Aria, "When Thou Art Near"
>> "Arioso"
>> "Jesu, Joy of Man's Desiring"
>> "Praise to the Lord, the Almighty"
>> Prelude in D
>> "Sarabande"
>> "Sheep May Safely Graze"
> Beethoven, L.
>> "Ode to Joy"
> Beillmann, L.
>> "Priere a' Notre Dame"
> Handel, G.F.
>> "Larghetto"
>> Selections From *Water Music Suite*

Liszt, F.
"Adagio"
Mendelssohn, F.
Excerpts From Organ Sonatas
Pachelbel, J.
"Cannon in D"
"Pastorale"
Peeters, F.
"Abide, O Dearest Jesus"
"Awake, My Heart, With Gladness"
"Ten Preludes on Old Flemish Tunes"

PROCESSIONALS

Bach, J.S.
Adagio in A Minor
"Symphonia From Wedding Cantata, 195"
Franck, C.
Fantasie in C
Handel, G.F.
"Andante Maestoso"
Aria From Concerto Grosso XII
Aria in F Major
Larghetto in F
Marcello, B.
"Psalm XIX"
"Psalm XX"
Purcell, H.
Largo in D Major
March in C
Trumpet Tune in D
Trumpet Voluntary in D

RECESSIONALS

Bach, J.S.
"In Thee Is Gladness"
"My Heart Ever Faithful"
Beethoven, L.
"Ode to Joy"
Doane, W.
"To God Be the Glory"
Dunstable, J.
"Agincourt Hymn"
Eldridge, G.H.
"Fanfare"
Goss, J.
"Praise My Soul, the King of Heaven"
Handel, G.F.
"Hallelujah Chorus"
Karg-Elert, S.
"Now Thank We All Our God"
Mendelssohn, F.
"War March of the Priests"
Purcell, H.
"Bell Symphony"
Trumpet Tune in C
Trumpet Tune in D Major
Trumpet Voluntary in D Major

HYMNS

"All Creatures of Our God and King," St. Francis of Assisi
"Be Thou My [Our] Vision," Ancient Irish
"Children of the Heavenly Father," Lina Sandell
"Day by Day," Lina Sandell Berg
"Fairest Lord Jesus," From the German
"For the Beauty of the Earth," F.S. Pierpoint

"God of Our Life, Through All the Circling Years,"
    Hugh T. Kerr
"Happy the Home," Henry Ware
"Joyful, Joyful We Adore Thee," Henry van Dyke
"Like a River Glorious," Frances Havergal
"Love Divine, All Loves Excelling," Charles Wesley
"May the Grace of Christ Our Saviour," John Newton
"May the Mind of Christ My [Our] Saviour," Kate B. Wilkinson
"Now Thank We All Our God," Martin Rinkart
"O Perfect Love," Dorothy Gurney
"Praise, My Soul, the King of Heaven," Henry F. Lyte
"Praise Ye the Lord, the Almighty," Joachim Neander
"Saviour, Like a Shepherd Lead Us," Dorothy A. Thrupp
"We Come, O Christ, to Thee," Margaret Clarkson
"We Rest on Thee," Edith G. Cherry

VOCAL MUSIC

"A Wedding Blessing," Austin Lovelace
"Be Thou With Them," J.S. Bach
"The Call," R. Vaughan-Williams
"Entreat Me Not to Leave Thee," C.F. Gounod
"The God of Love My Shepherd Is," E. Thiman
"The Greatest of These Is Love," R. Bitgood
"Here at Thine Altar, Lord," A. Rowley
"If With All Your Hearts," F. Mendelssohn
"Jesu, Joy of Man's Desiring," J.S. Bach
"Jesus, Lead Our Footsteps Ever," J.S. Bach
"Jesus, Shepherd, Be Thou Near Me," J.S. Bach
"The King of Love My Shepherd Is," Bairstow
"Like a Shepherd God Doth Lead Us," J.S. Bach
"The Lord's Prayer," Regina H. Fryxell; also Ley
"Love Divine," B. Marcello
"My Heart, Ever Faithful," J.S. Bach
"O Perfect Love" Leo Sowerby; also J.B. Clokey

"O Lord Most Holy," Caesar Franck
"O Love That Casts Out Fear," J.S. Bach
"Oh, Blest the House Whate're Befall," Henry Markworth
"Psalm 150," Ned Rorem
"Set Me as a Seal Upon Thine Heart," Joseph Clokey
"Thou Wilt Keep Him in Perfect Peace," E. Thiman
"Though I Speak With the Tongues," J. Brahms
"We Lift Our Hearts to Thee," A. Lovelace
"Wedding Song," H. Schultz
"Whither Thou Goest," G. Winston Cassler

14
Showers and Gifts

Never in your life will you enjoy so many parties! Before the wedding many friends and relatives will want to entertain you and your fiancé. Watch your calendar carefully, however. Too much partying can be tiring and can rob you of valuable time spent with each other. Thoughtful friends will understand if you tactfully suggest a rain check for after the wedding.

Showers may be given by anyone except immediate members of your family or your fiancé's family. Be sure that your fiancé, your mother, or best friend knows your schedule so one of them can suggest the best times to hostesses who might ask. If you know that surprise parties could unbalance your emotional equilibrium, tell your fiancé who can pass along the word to any surprise-party throwers.

If the hostess asks what type of shower you want, feel free to state your preference: personal, kitchen, linen, whatever. Showers these days are no longer limited to women. Your fiancé might like to be invited to help open the gifts and share the festivities. Or someone might like to give a co-ed shower to which his friends are also invited.

Thank each giver as you open each gift. In addition it's nice (though not demanded) to send written thanks. Always write a note to the hostess, thanking her for giving the party.

Wedding Gifts

Receiving gifts is one of the joys of getting married. Each gift represents not only someone's affection for you, but also their faith that your marriage will be truly happy and enduring.

Gift registry: You probably have some ideas about the gifts that you would like to receive. And your friends would appreciate knowing your preferences. Most department stores have a free wedding-gift service that lets you register your choices so your friends can select gifts they know you want. A consultant will be glad to help you look at china, crystal, and silver or stainless and can make suggestions about combining patterns, should you need her help. She also knows which companies deliver quickly, and which keep their patterns open for longer periods of time.

Before going to register, decide with your fiancé on the colors you'll want in your bath and bedroom. Also decide what size bed you will want (*see* chapter 29) and the size dining table you are likely to use.

Then take a shopping trip together to see china, silver, and crystal patterns. If, like many modern brides, you prefer pottery and stainless, look at those. Take time to think through your choices, for you'll be using them for years to come. In fact, you probably won't decide on your first trip.

When you have made your decisions, register at the major department stores in both your hometown and your fiancé's. Most stores will also list your choices for electrical appliances, kitchenware, cookware, and entertaining accessories. Be sure to list a number of moderately priced choices.

Some stores automatically check off each gift purchased for you. Other stores depend on the bride to telephone when she has received gifts from her list. Be sure and ask.

Recording your gifts: As soon as each gift arrives, open it carefully. If it arrives damaged, call or write the store at once. If the gift was wrapped by the giver and not insured, send your thanks without mentioning the damage.

Record all gifts immediately. You may use your card file for this. Or better yet, use a notebook or wedding memory book that has space for recording gifts. Your listing should include this information:

DATE   GIFT   GIVEN BY   THANKS WRITTEN

For gifts received at the wedding, have someone tape each card to its package. Should cards and gifts become separated, you'll need to ask delicately whether the card was attached to a gift. Never imply either by tone of voice or facial expression that you expected a gift.

Thank-you notes: You must acknowledge each gift with a personal note—as quickly as possible. All thank-you notes should be written within three months of the wedding. Start writing your notes as soon as the first gifts arrive, and keep up as best you can. Before the wedding, use plain note paper or paper monogrammed with your maiden initials. After the wedding, you may use note paper with your married monogram.

Although cards with printed messages are available, these are impersonal and unacceptable. Anyone who took the time and expense to select a gift deserves your warm, personal thanks.

Make your thank-you notes sound like you. Be casual and conversational. Stereotyped letters are not worth reading, because you know exactly what they are going to say. Always mention the gift, and tell how you will use it. Better yet, whenever possible express your appreciation for what that person has meant to you. For example:

> Dear Lisa,
> John and I are so pleased to receive a cup and saucer for
> our china collection. How special that it should come

from you! I'll always remember our coffee breaks together. I deeply appreciate your willingness to listen to and encourage me, and for sharing some of the secrets that give you and Dave such a happy marriage. I'm sure our marriage will be richer for our talks together.

Lovingly,
Jean

Although note writing used to be solely the bride's duty, more and more grooms are sharing the responsibility.

Exchanging gifts: It's inevitable that you will receive some duplicates, or some gifts that you cannot use. This calls for some discretion. Exact duplicates can be exchanged easily. If the giver is not likely to visit, or his gift would not be readily seen (a blanket or kitchen appliance, for example), these may be returned. Otherwise, it is better to keep and use the gift than to offend the giver.

After the wedding, separate any gifts to be exchanged. Keep them in their original boxes with any stickers or other indication of the store where they were purchased. Most stores will exchange only the gifts that were purchased there.

Displaying your gifts: If you have the time and inclination, displaying your gifts for friends to admire is a pleasant custom. In days gone by, every bride displayed her gifts. Friends would pay a visit, bring their gifts, and view the other gifts received. But with more brides and their mothers working, few want so many visitors during the final hectic weeks before the wedding.

You can cover card tables with cloths and artistically arrange your gifts. If you feel more extravagant, you might rent tables and long skirts. Tactfully separate similar gifts. If you receive a duplicate, display only one. Display only one place setting of your china, crystal, and silver.

Displaying cards to indicate who sent each gift is your

choice. Some enjoy showing who sent what. Others feel this invites comparisons. Do not show the amounts of checks or gift certificates, however. Either overlap them so that only the signatures show, with a pretty paperweight hiding the first amount, or write on a card: *Check from Uncle Dick and Aunt Harriet.*

Insuring the gifts: Although none of your friends would steal anything, many deliverymen will be coming. A theft at this time can be more upsetting than usual. Most insurance companies issue short-term policies called floaters to cover the gifts until you move into your new home.

Your Gratitude

In thanksgiving to God, who will unite you in marriage and has abundantly blessed you with friends and gifts, you might want to give a special thank offering to your church or a mission project. Perhaps you could write your first check from your joint account, symbolic of giving God your firstfruits. As you form the pattern of giving first to God, you will be blessed.

15
What's in a Name?

Today when you become legally linked to your husband, you have several options for your married name.

Use your husband's last name: This, of course, is the traditional way. You'll sign checks and legal papers as first name, maiden name, husband's last name. *Debra Sue Johnson* becomes *Debra Johnson Long.* If you wish, you may retain you middle name: *Debra Sue Long.*

Form a combined last name: You may choose to use a hyphenated name: *Debra Johnson-Long.* Your husband would also legally change his name to include your maiden name: *Thomas Johnson-Long.*

Keep your maiden name: It is now acceptable to retain your maiden name. Thus you would be *Debra Johnson* married to *Thomas Long.* Although legal, this can cause confusion. If you have established your career in your maiden name, you might keep that name professionally but legally and socially take your husband's name.

In signing business letters you will be: *Debra Long (Mrs. Thomas).* Or *Debra Johnson Long.* But never *Mrs. Debra Long.* To your friends, you'll always be *Debra.*

For monograms, use the first initial of your first name, the initial of your maiden name, and the first initial of your married name—the latter being the largest. Or (more informal) use a large initial of your married name centered between the initials of your first name and your husband's first name.

$\mathcal{D}\mathcal{L}J$ OR $\mathcal{D}J\mathcal{L}$ $\mathcal{D}\mathcal{L}T$

Establishing Your Identity

Marriage is a joyful celebration. But it is also a legal change of name and status, and that means paperwork. Some legal papers you can care for before the wedding. Others, such as driver's license and social security, may require a certified copy of your marriage certificate. Here are some of the name changes and legal matters to which you must attend.

Bank accounts: You may open joint savings and/or checking accounts with your fiancé a few weeks before the wedding. The account will read: Gerald Allen Long or Phyllis Mosher Morgan (also known as Phyllis Mosher or Mrs. Gerald Long). This arrangement allows you to transact business both before and after the wedding.

Magazine subscriptions: Send notice of your change of name and address six to eight weeks before the wedding.

Charge accounts: Send notice in writing of your new name and address. You can also instruct creditors to add your new husband's signature to your accounts, and he can do the same for you on his accounts.

Postal service: Give a forwarding address (in both your maiden and married names) to begin after the wedding.

Board of voter registration: Send written notice either before or after your wedding. If you move to another community, register to vote there.

Car registration: Send written notice either before or after the wedding.

Employment office: Give notice before the wedding, and change your deduction status with the Internal Revenue Service.

School records: Send your new information to any schools from which you have graduated to update records, or to the registration office if you are still in school.

Insurance: Change the name of beneficiaries on all policies to become effective the day of the wedding. If you have no household insurance, take out a policy to cover your wedding gifts and furnishings. Be sure you have adequate health insurance as well.

Wills: No one likes to contemplate death—especially before a wedding! But the wise couple will meet with a lawyer before their wedding and draw up their wills. Should anything happen to either of you, the other would be saved much grief and inconvenience not to mention legal expense if you have a will.

Social Security: You must present a certified copy of your marriage certificate and your Social Security card to make this change.

Driver's license: Check local requirements, but you usually are required to go in person with a certified copy of your marriage certificate.

16
The Rehearsal

Even if you've attended and participated in many weddings, you'll need to rehearse your own. Besides being fun, the rehearsal gives you and your wedding party the confidence of knowing all the cues and procedures and gives you an opportunity to work out any rough spots. The best-made plans on paper can have details dangling that become evident only as you walk through the ceremony.

Who should be included? Invite all members of the wedding party, the minister(s), musicians, ushers, and parents. Spouses and out-of-town relatives may be included as spectators.

When should the rehearsal be held? Although the rehearsal is usually held the evening before the wedding, it could be scheduled two or three days in advance if all attendants are in town. This added time allows you to work out any details without panic, and also allows you to have a much more relaxing evening before your wedding. If the rehearsal must take place the evening before the wedding, schedule it as early as possible. You'll need a good night's rest.

What decisions must be made? Before the rehearsal you and the groom should go through all the details with your minister. From his experience he can make many suggestions that will help your rehearsal (and wedding) progress smoothly. Have him evaluate your wedding-day schedule.

107

Decide now which aisles you will use if the church has no center aisle. Will ushers walk with the bridesmaids or enter from the vestry? During the recessional will they walk in pairs or single file? Do you prefer each bridesmaid to take her usher's arm or for him to extend his forearm, her hand resting on his? Will you use a slow, natural walk down the aisle or the hesitation step?

Do you wish the congregation to stand or remain seated when you enter? (If the church has no center aisle, you will not be able to see your groom if they stand.)

Will you take your father's right or left arm? It's easier if you take his right so that he doesn't have to cross in back of you to reach his seat.

Do you plan to kiss your mother during the processional and his during the recessional? Or greet both sets of parents during the recessional? Or give roses from your bouquet to the mothers? Plan now how you will do this.

What will be the exact order of your processional? The traditional order for both processional and recessional follows. Feel free to suggest variations. Where will the wedding-party members stand during the ceremony? Do you plan to have part of the ceremony while standing at the end of the aisle, then move into the chancel? Plan exactly when you will do this.

Will ushers ask guests whether they are friends of the bride or groom? Or will they fill each side equally? Will you have any special seating arrangements?

Your minister should know all your decisions on these questions. He then will take charge at your rehearsal and can deal tactfully with any parent or other members of the wedding party who try to impose their plans. He'll also make certain that everyone involved knows the timing and cues. Organist and musicians must know when to begin the processional and when to begin any music planned during the ceremony. Be sure, also, that the organist knows the cue for the recessional lest he begin too soon.

When you have made all your decisions, make a wedding-day schedule to be distributed at your rehearsal. This insures that everyone involved knows when they are to arrive and what they are to do.

Do you believe in superstition? Tradition says it's bad luck for a bride to rehearse her own wedding. But that's never been proven. And it really could be disastrous if you haven't rehearsed your pace and positions. So phooey on superstition—and enjoy your rehearsal.

Be sure to bring your marriage certificate to give the minister. As much as possible, bring all the items needed on your wedding day: service bulletins, matches to light the candles, ribbons for the pews, and so on.

The Rehearsal Dinner

This is usually held immediately following the rehearsal. If the rehearsal might run late, however, consider scheduling dinner first. Your attendants will be much more congenial with full stomachs!

Often the groom's family hosts this dinner, but your parents or other relatives may do the honors. It can be held at home, in a restaurant, or in the church basement (left clean, of course). Plan the type of dinner that suits you and your families, whether a formal dinner with place cards and centerpieces, or pizza, Chinese food, a catered barbecue, or picnic.

All the members of the wedding party, their spouses, and both sets of parents must be invited. You may also invite the minister and his wife, out-of-town guests, and other special friends.

The groom should act as master of ceremonies, welcoming everyone, making introductions if necessary, and arranging for someone to begin the meal with prayer. Your parents might want to have their last words, telling those funny stories from your childhood.

If you have not planned separate bachelor and bridesmaids' parties, for your attendants, now is a nice time to distribute your thank-you gifts to them.

Processional

Bride   Father

Flower Girl

Ring Bearer

Maid of Honor

Bridesmaid

Bridesmaid

Usher Usher Best Man Groom

Minister

OR

Bride   Father

Flower Girl

Ring Bearer

Maid of Honor

Bridesmaid

Bridesmaid

Usher

Usher

Best Man   Groom

Minister

NOTE: Bridesmaids may walk in twos if there are four or more. Or ushers may escort bridesmaids in both processional and recessional.

Recessional

Minister

Bridesmaid	Usher
Bridesmaid	Usher
Maid of Honor	Best Man
Flower Girl	Ring Bearer
Bride	Groom

Sample Wedding-Day Schedule

11:30   Bride and bridesmaids arrive to dress; bride's parents arrive

12:00   Groom, best man, ushers, groom's immediate family arrive. Photos taken of bridal party and families. Time for snack.

1:15   Ministers arrive for photos and final instructions

1:30   Ushers (those not standing up for wedding) arrive for photos

1:45   Musicians arrive (ushers get ready)

2:00   Prelude begins

2:30   Ushers light candles

Seat groom's parents

Vocal solo

Seat late-comers

Seat bride's mother

Lay aisle runner

Processional begins

17
The Jitters

You *will* have them! At some time every bride does. The wise bride allows for these emotions in her planning. Leave yourself enough leeway so you can take it easy when the jitters hit.

The jitters fall into two categories. The first is stress. Every change—even good change—brings stress. That stress will express itself in anger, anxiety, or fatigue. Because marriage is one of the biggest changes you'll ever experience—with one of the highest stress ratings—you will probably find yourself overreacting to minor irritations and mishaps. You may explode at your fiancé or mother over nothing. You may develop ridiculous anxieties (What if the cake topples? What if I trip?). Or your normal energy may evaporate, leaving you with extreme fatigue.

Don't worry!

If at all possible talk to another engaged girl or recent bride. It helps to know that your reactions are normal. Remember that you are under stress, so be kind to yourself. Don't demand a bionic performance. If at all possible, rest for fifteen or twenty minutes each day. Especially if you are working full-time, don't schedule wedding preparations every evening. Give yourself time to relax.

Continue eating a balanced diet at regular mealtimes. You may be tempted to eat on the run, which usually means junk food with a minimum of fruits and vegetables. Don't! This regime will leave your body weak and your nerves more frazzled. If signs of stress seem especially acute, see your physician.

The second category of jitters revolves around your life-long marriage commitment. You might find yourself afraid to take that step. After all, you know how to live as a single person. But what will it mean to be bound to another? You wonder how you and your fiancé would cope with a financial reversal, a handicap, a serious accident. You may exaggerate the consequences of any difficulty in your relationship. Or you may experience a nebulous fear that hangs like a dark cloud.

The "White Panic"

"Expect the white panic," one newlywed told me when I became engaged. "The books never tell you this, but you'll probably wake up in the middle of the night wondering, 'What on earth am I doing?'"

"Be not afraid of sudden fear . . ." the Bible says in Proverbs 3:25. This means my friend's "white panic" that strikes at an odd hour. Commit that fear to the Lord and claim His peace. "I sought the Lord and he heard me, and delivered me from all my fears," David says in Psalms 34:4. If your fear is nothing more than "white panic," it will pass.

If, however, your fear is very specific, you need to work through the problem with your fiancé. If you have a serious difference that you cannot reconcile, talk with your pastor or a professional counselor. Believe it or not, problems are much easier to solve before you marry.

You'll also find that you don't feel engulfing romantic love at all times. This, too, is entirely normal. Such feelings are nice when they come. But they're not the foundation for marriage. If you truly believe this commitment to be God's will, continue to show 1 Corinthians 13 love to your fiancé, and the feelings will return. In the process you'll mature in unselfish love—the best kind to bring into marriage.

Handling the Wedding-Day Jitters

Then there are those wedding-day jitters. Whatever panic your mind may suggest, ignore it completely. If you have been sure until now, you're sure. Tell a trusted friend and laugh about it together. Then go ahead and enjoy your big day.

Your wedding day will be more jitter free if you have done a thorough job of planning and preparing. Aim for an easy, relaxed morning free of responsibility.

And take time to eat!

Your adrenalin will be flowing, and your blood sugar disappearing. So by all means eat breakfast, and have at least a light snack before the wedding. One bride, a registered nurse, left so many details for her wedding day that she had no time to eat. She whirled nonstop until time to walk the aisle. She finished the details. But as she started to repeat her vows, she fainted. Her groom and minister propped her up, wisely injecting a prayer, until someone brought a glass of water. And the wedding continued.

Be prepared. And may you be a happy, relaxed bride!

Murphy's Law

You've heard it, of course: "Whatever can go wrong, will go wrong at the worst possible moment."

This rule doesn't apply to weddings!

If everything goes as planned, you'll be grateful. Any minor mishaps can be rescued, and few will notice. What if something major happens? Then you've guaranteed that *nobody* will forget your wedding! And you'll be retelling the story for years, laughing every time.

If you've been to a number of weddings, which do you remember best?

Two weddings stand out in my memory. At one, the entire bridal party had been exposed to the flu. But it hit the groom worst of all. When he walked out with the minister, he looked green. As the ceremony began, the minister made a discreet hand signal to the organist, then placed his hands on the couple's shoulders. After a brief prayer, thanking God for their marriage, he sent them down the aisle without vows or further ado. And just in time! After a rest, they formed a receiving line with the groom sitting on a chair. Now years later friends still tease them about making no promises to each other.

Another wedding took place on a hot Texas evening. The couple had rented a small chapel near their home. That afternoon the groom checked to see that all was in order. But alas, the janitor had forgotten to unlock the church. The pastor was away on vacation, and the couple had no other number to call. Undaunted, the groom tested all the windows, then in desperation climbed a drain spout to unlock a second-story window. He succeeded in opening all necessary doors—all, that is, except the front door.

With the front door locked, the bride would have to enter from the side. That she refused. When nothing else worked, she and her bridesmaids jumped through a small front window—large hoop skirt and all. And the wedding proceeded.

When the couple began their honeymoon, they discovered the newspapers had gotten a photo of the bride jumping through the window, making front pages across their part of the country. Everywhere they traveled, they were recognized, with restaurants giving them free meals and strangers wishing them well.

Murphy's law? Never! Little things might upset your wedding plans, but nothing needs to upset your marriage.

18
Your Wedding Service

For years nobody questioned the traditional wedding service. Brides marched the aisle to *Lohengrin,* repeated age-old vows, and marched out to Mendelssohn's "Wedding March." But how many seriously thought through their service or their vows?

Then came the innovative weddings, when it seemed almost a rule that every couple *must* write their vows and do something original. Weddings took place in hang gliders and on horseback. Promises were made "as long as we both shall love." These ceremonies, though original, often contained more sentiment than deep commitment.

Today, you are free to be as traditional or as innovative as you wish. Since you probably will get married only once, make the service special, something you will remember. Make it as worshipful and holy as marriage itself.

Think through each part of the service. You may discover you *want* to retain at least some traditions. Wedding rituals link you with the past and reaffirm the continuity of marriage from one generation to the next. You may find Elizabethan language beautiful and the vows lofty. And there is a sense of history in knowing that for hundreds of years couples have said these words.

You may find some parts of the traditional wedding service meaningless. If so, feel free to eliminate or change them. If you find the giving away outmoded, or if the question of whether anyone knows "any just cause" against the marriage to "speak now or else hereafter forever hold his peace" seems perfunctory, then change these parts or any others that do not seem to fit.

Take nothing in the service for granted. Don't accept tradition just because it's tradition. But don't make changes just to be different or to show off. Whatever you plan, the service should reflect your Christian values. Your service should be as precious and individual as your love, and it should reflect the seriousness with which you regard marriage.

Important Questions to Ask Yourselves

Before planning your service, ask yourselves some important questions:

> What do we want to accomplish?
> What values do we want to communicate?
> What is important to us?

The more fully you can answer these questions, the easier the remaining decisions will be.

Your wedding service should reflect a blend of your values and personalities. Neither should dominate the decisions. Plan together and work through any differences in a productive way. Learn to accept the creativity of each and to express your opinion without squelching the other. This process will give you valuable patterns to take into marriage. If you come from two cultures, plan a wedding that will reflect both.

Learn, also, to work with both families. Communication is the key. Although the two of you are responsible for planning your service, keep communicating with your parents. Tell them your plans, and ask their advice when you want it. Mothers especially like to feel included. Begin a good relationship by telephoning or writing to your new mother-in-law and keeping her informed of the proceedings.

If either family tries to dominate your plans, you'll need the wisdom of Solomon and the tact of a diplomat. The most joyous weddings are those in which both families are congenial and cooperative. Sadly, this is not always true. Ask God for the grace to be both wise and loving. Work with your fiancé in handling the situation together. Try to begin good patterns of relating to both families. Although you don't want to let anyone pressure you into plans you don't want, beware of exaggerating small disagreements. If you must turn down a suggestion, be kind and appreciative.

One bride set a goal to reduce tensions and to build good relationships. She wrote her future mother-in-law weekly, beginning a friendship that has endured. She tried to keep a jump ahead in planning so her own mother wouldn't feel obligated to take on extra work. Their love deepened during the wedding-planning days.

Another bride's mother so interfered with wedding plans that the bride vowed she would never visit home after the wedding.

"Honey," her fiancé wisely advised, "these are the most important people in the world to us. And we're not going to let anything break our relationship with them. We're going to love them so much they have no choice but to love us back." And that's just what happened.

Use your wedding-planning days to build, not destroy, important relationships. "The wise woman builds her house, But the foolish tears it down with her own hands" (Proverbs 14:1 NAS).

When you're ready to begin planning your service, inform your minister. He may have a contemporary service in his handbook. Both a traditional and a contemporary service are included in following chapters. You may wish to write your own service. If so, work closely with your minister.

However you plan your service, it will probably include some or most of the following elements. You may want to add features, or to rearrange the parts. But each section should give you some idea starters. Keep in mind your values and the purposes you want your wedding to achieve, and try to make each part of the service express meaning.

Prelude

Usually, the music begins about thirty minutes before the service. This music sets the mood for your wedding and encourages guests to enter worshipfully. Your organist will be glad to supply the prelude music, and probably has many selections to suggest. Go over these, however, and choose the ones you like best. You might want all classical or all hymns, or a combination. (*See* music guide in chapter 13.)

Do you have musicians available among your friends or family? Someone who plays flute, recorder, violin, cello, harp, or guitar could be asked to play a few selections.

Use the piano rather than the organ. Or provide taped contemporary Christian music.

Processional

Because of the secular nature of Wagner's "Bridal Chorus" and Mendelssohn's "Wedding March," they have fallen from popularity in recent years. And few want their guests filling in the words, "Here comes the bride, big, fat and wide!"

See the music suggestions for a wide range of possibilities. Your organist might have several of these or other selections for you to listen to and choose.

You might use a congregational hymn for your entry. This helps guests focus on worship.

Or have someone (even your groom, if he sings) sing as you come down the aisle.

Some feel that the traditional processional dramatizes the beauty of the bride, supported by family and best friends, coming to meet her groom. Others, however, feel conspicuous in the spotlight. If you're one of these, think of an alternative.

Each family could form a processional, escorting bride and groom. Or, if a father or brother is not available, your minister could escort you down the aisle.

One bride sat on the first pew of the left side, and the groom on the first pew of the right. After a call to worship and prayer, the minister simply said, "Will the bride and groom please come forward."

Another bride had her wedding as part of the Sunday-evening service. They wanted their marriage to be part of a worship service rather than a ceremony. No ushers were needed, since people normally seat themselves for this service. The bride, with her family and attendants, sat on the left, and groom, with his family and attendants, sat on the right. After the congregational hymns, prayer, and message, they stepped forward to be married.

Another bride, whose family did not attend the wedding, had the groom and ushers enter from the vestry. As each bridesmaid started down the aisle, the usher walked to meet her halfway and escort her to the front of the church. The groom, however, walked the entire length of the aisle to escort his bride. Marriage, they implied, is never fifty-fifty. They would walk all the way through life together.

One bride, whose church had very long aisles, chose instead the enter from the balcony. She and the groom formed a pleasing pageant by walking slowly down the stairs—she on the left side and he on the right—that led to the chancel.

You may choose an evening wedding. After guests are seated, dim all the lights while members of the bridal party take their places. Have a spotlight focus first on the groom reading a passage of Scripture. Then focus a second spotlight on you, reading another passage. Or have played the "Morning" theme from Grieg's *Peer Gynt Suite* or "Morning Has Broken" as the lights are gradually increased.

Call to Worship

Your pastor will probably begin the service by welcoming the guests and inviting them to worship. He may use Scripture (suggest favorite verses if you like). Or you could have a parent extend this call, or several people prearranged to rise from the congregation to read short verses or short Scripture portions.

Charge to the Couple

Traditional ceremonies offer first the couple, then the members of the congregation, the opportunity to express any reason why the two should not be married. Some appreciate this formal way of demonstrating their legal right to marry.

Prayer

Usually the minister at this point will pray, asking God's blessing on the wedding service and on the couple. You may choose, however, to have members of your wedding party or your family offer this prayer.

Declaration of Consent

The minister now asks both bride and groom if they will have this woman/man as their husband/wife. This tradition allows each to state his intention to marry and be faithful with an "I will" or, as one couple answered, "I certainly will!"

You may choose to add a further statement about your faith in Christ by having the minister first ask each of you, "Have you received Jesus Christ as your Lord and Saviour? And do you believe this marriage to be His will?" As you publicly answer, you witness that the most important decision in your life is to receive Christ, and that He as Lord now directs your decisions.

Giving Away

Traditionally, the minister asks, "Who gives this woman to be married to this man?" Her father responds, "I do" or "Her mother and I do." Although this custom dates back to the days of dowry, many retain it as symbolic of leaving father and mother. It also acknowledges the parents' responsibility for their child. Before making any changes in this custom, discuss your alternatives with your father. He may be looking forward to this role!

If your father is deceased or unable to attend, you could have an older brother or uncle do the honors. Or you could walk the aisle alone, having your mother stand at the appropriate time to say, "I do."

You could have the pastor invite parents of both bride and groom to stand. He then asks them, "Will you, parents of this man and woman, give your blessings to their union?" To which they answer, "We do."

If both sets of parents are Christians, he could say, "You have acknowledged that children are a heritage from the Lord, and you have faithfully given of yourselves to bring these, your children, up in the nurture and admonition of the Lord.

"As they stand before you this day, do you recognize the leading of God in their lives? And do you now enter into their joy, giving your blessing to their union?"

Some couples then have the pastor address the congregation. He asks, "All of you who witness their vows, will you do everything in your power to support and uphold these two persons in their marriage? Then say, 'We will!' "

You could use this point in the service to recognize God's giving you to each other. The minister—or your father or escort—could answer the traditional question with: "Mark and Mary believe that 'every good gift and every perfect gift is from above, and comes down from the Father of lights.' " (*See* James 1:17.)

19
Scripture Readings

You may include Scripture at any number of places in the ceremony. Use it for your call to worship. Have a Scripture reading before the pastor's meditation. Use Scripture as a prayer or as a response.

Although you may have the minister read Scripture, you could allow others to participate. Have one or more parents read it. Have your bridal party or best man read your selections. Have the congregation read in unison or responsively.

If individuals read Scripture, encourage them to practice until they can read expressively. Never allow the reading of Scripture to become a boring drone or mumble.

One bride had her father read 1 Corinthians 13 before being seated beside her mother. Another couple had the bride's father read an Old Testament portion, and the groom's father, a New Testament portion. You could have the members of your wedding party read Scripture selections. Or have several assigned from the congregation to rise and read Scripture passages about marriage and love. To heighten the effectiveness, have each reader begin his verse as the previous reader finishes his last three or four words. This eliminates dead silences, and the ear can pick up both.

Either your pastor or your parents can give a short meditation on the meaning of marriage in Scripture, the beauty of having Christ in your home, or words of wisdom for the two of you to take into your new life. At one wedding each father wrote *A Letter to My Son* or *A Letter to My Daughter* which the pastor read at this point.

You want your marriage to be a witness to those who do not know Jesus Christ as Saviour. The best witness will probably be a deeply worshipful service rather than an evangelistic message. Let the beauty of Christ be seen. Clearly state what it means to belong to Christ, but don't use this time to preach.

Selecting Scripture

As Christians, our guide for marriage comes solely from Scripture. Although we recognize the wisdom of counselors and the vast resources available through both Christian and secular books, these are not our final authority. Only by carefully studying and obeying the wisdom of Scripture can our marriages have the beauty that God intends. As one Christian marriage counselor says, "You are the student, your mate is your subject, the Bible is your textbook, the Holy Spirit is your teacher, and your marriage is your laboratory." That study will never end!

Marriage, the traditional wedding service declares, is to be entered "in the fear of the Lord." The Bible adds that "The fear of the Lord is the beginning of wisdom . . ." (Proverbs 9:10). Where does that wisdom come from? "For the Lord gives wisdom, and from his mouth come knowledge and understanding" (Proverbs 2:6 NIV). Look at the benefit to your home. "By wisdom a house is built, and through understanding it is established; through knowledge its rooms are filled with rare and beautiful treasures" (Proverbs 24:3, 4 NIV).

If you have not already done so, begin studying God's Word together. Read aloud the Song of Solomon until its inspired phrases of love become your own. Study together the Book of Proverbs, discussing how you can put its wisdom

to use in your life. Study the Scriptures about love and marriage listed here.

After reading and studying these Scriptures, select some
of your favorites to be included in your wedding. Look at
several translations to select the wording that seems clearest
to you. If either of you have other favorite verses, you may
include these also, even if they do not specifically relate to
marriage.

By including Scripture in your wedding, you are affirming
that your direction in life comes from God's Word. You are
encouraging your guests to adopt God's view of the beauty
of marriage rather than the cynical view of the world. You
are also directing their praise and worship.

Here is a list of Scripture passages that could be used.
Some, not specifically about love or marriage, direct praise
to God—a praise you will feel deeply on your wedding day.

Old Testament Readings

Genesis 1:26, 27: Creation of man
Genesis 2:18, 21–24: Creation of woman
Genesis 24:48–51, 58–67: Marriage of Isaac and Rebekah
Ruth 1:16, 17: "Entreat me not to leave thee. . . ."
Psalms 29:1, 2: "Give unto the Lord glory. . . .'"
Psalms 34:3: "O magnify the Lord with me. . . ."
Psalms 63:1–4: "O God, thou art my God. . . ."
Psalms 95:1–6: "O come, let us sing unto the Lord. . . ."
Psalms 100: "Make a joyful noise unto the Lord. . . ."
Psalms 127: "Except the Lord build the house. . . ."
Psalms 128: "Blessed is every one that feareth the Lord. . . ."
Psalms 150: "Praise God in his sanctuary . . . ."
Proverbs 5:15–19: "Drink waters out of thine own cistern. . . ."
Proverbs 18:22: "Whoso findeth a wife. . . ."
Proverbs 24:3, 4: Foundation of a home
Proverbs 31:10–31: "Who can find a virtuous woman?"

Ecclesiastes 4:9–12: "Two are better than one. . . ."
Song of Solomon 2:11–13: "For, lo, the winter is past. . . ."
Song of Solomon 6:3: "I am my beloved's. . . ."
Song of Solomon 5:16: "This is my beloved, and this is my
friend. . . ."
Song of Solomon 8:6, 7: "Set me as a seal. . . ."
Isaiah 61:10: "I will greatly rejoice in the Lord. . . ."
Isaiah 62:5: "For as a young man marrieth a virgin. . . ."
Jeremiah 33:11: "The voice of joy, and the voice of
gladness. . . ."
Hosea 2:19, 20: "And I will betroth thee unto me for ever. . . ."

New Testament Readings

Matthew 5:3–11: Beatitudes
Matthew 19:4–6: Christ's statement on marriage
John 2:1–11: Christ at the marriage in Cana
John 15:9–17: Christ's command to love
John 17:22, 23: Christ's prayer for love and unity
1 Corinthians 7:1–7: Marital duty of husband and wife
• 1 Corinthians 13: Great love chapter
Ephesians 5:21–33: Roles of husband and wife
Philippians 2:5–11: Attitudes to build marriage
Hebrews 13:4: Sex in marriage
1 Peter 3:1–7: Teaching for wives and husbands
1 John 3:16; 4:7–19: Teachings on love

20
Exchanging Vows and Rings

A friend, to be married in a week, told me excitedly about her dress, her flowers, her reception. "And what vows are you using?" I asked.

"Oh, that's right! We haven't really done much about vows. I guess we'll use the traditional ones."

Although each element of wedding preparation is important and must be done, nothing is more important than the vows you make to one another, for these are your promises for a lifetime. Think carefully about the commitment you're making and discuss together the meaning of each promise. When you stand before the congregation to make your pledge, you'll know the sincere thought that went into each statement. On your wedding day you may be too excited to comprehend what you're saying, but you'll know that these promises come from your heart.

Whether you choose to write your own vows or to use the traditional ones, think carefully about each phrase, projecting its meaning into the future.

Wedding promises are so easy to say, yet so difficult to live out. When I first wrote my vows, I felt tempted to rip the paper. How could I possibly keep such promises for twenty-four hours, much less a lifetime? How much more realistic, I thought, just to say, "I love you, and will try my best to be a good wife." Yet how much better to verbalize the ideals.

Even though we know we will fail, we express the love we want to have and the person we want to be by God's grace.

Writing Your Vows

If you write your own vows, first think through several categories, making rough notes on each. You may want to consider the following questions.

What promises from the traditional vows do you wish to retain? These vows contain the wisdom gained through years of use, so consider them seriously. You may want to restate the principles in your own words, but preserve their wisdom. The vows acknowledge that a new relationship begins today. They also acknowledge life's unknowns. No couple entering marriage knows whether they will encounter sickness, job loss, accident, disappointment. But true love, according to God's holy ordinance, makes its commitment regardless of circumstances.

What does Scripture say about marriage, about love, about the roles of husband and wife? Study the Scriptures listed in chapter 19 and list God's requirements. Then incorporate these into your vows.

What do you mean when you say, "I love you"? Put your personal statement into your vows.

What qualities do you most appreciate in each other? One couple talked together about the characteristics that first attracted them. The groom promised to make his bride laugh—a vow he's kept for ten years. Find out what your loved one adores in you, then vow to preserve those attributes.

How do you want to help your fiancé and to keep your marriage healthy? Incorporate some of the wisdom you've gained through premarital counseling, and promise to keep your marriage a loving, growing one.

Now that you have listed the promises that are most important to you, write a rough draft of your vows. Read it aloud, and make any changes needed to give it rhythm and flow. Are any sentences or phrases too long to speak in one breath? Shorten the wording or divide the statement into two sentences. Do some of the phrases sound wordy? Cut out any extras. Keep reading over your vows for several days until you are sure this is what you want to promise.

You and your fiancé should work through your vows individually, so that each is thinking through his/her responsibilities in marriage. When each has written rough drafts, share them with each other, explaining what you mean. You may then choose to use your vows as you've written them, or you may revise them so that they are parallel in structure and content.

Several examples of original vows follow. Although you probably won't want to use them verbatim, you may find their ideas helpful.

When you have completed your vows, you may choose to memorize them, to repeat them phrase by phrase after your minister, or to read them to each other. Memorizing is the most personal, but this adds extra anxiety to an already exciting day. If you get tense, better choose another option. Reading your vows provides a good alternative. Type copies of your vows and tie or staple them into white folders. Your minister can then hand these to you at the appropriate time.

During the wedding service, the groom gives his vows first, followed by the bride. You may give your rings as part of your vows, or you may make this a separate act.

One couple had the groom give his vows, followed by a vocalist singing a song he had chosen to express his love. The bride then gave her vows, followed by a song of her choice.

After the wedding, keep permanent copies of your vows to read on anniversaries. One couple had a friend print their vows on eleven-by-fourteen paper, which they framed and hung in the bedroom. One groom framed a typed copy and keeps it on his desk beside his bride's picture—a constant reminder of his promises to her.

21
Sample Vows

Because God has favored me by bringing you into my life, a helper that fits perfectly, I take you, Kay, to be my lawful wedded wife according to God's holy ordinance. I promise to be faithful, placing you as a seal over my heart and on my arm, finding satisfaction and joy only in you.

I will strive to live with you in an understanding way, giving you the honor due you as an heir together of the grace of life. I will seek for our marriage to be one of harmony, sympathy, sacrificial love, compassion, and humility, both in times of abundance and happiness, and in times of adversity, knowing that our life together is entrusted to our faithful Creator.

My love is committed to you for as long as we both shall live—a love by God's grace that will be patient and kind, without envy or boasting, pride or rudeness; a love that will not be selfish or easily angered or keep record of wrongs; a love that delights in right and truth, always protecting, trusting, hoping, and enduring. This love, the very flame of the Lord, by His strength will not be quenched.

As your leader and head, I will nurture and cherish you as my own self, giving you the care, support, and encouragement you need to help you fulfill your potential and be all the woman our Lord intended you to be. Through-

out our life together, you are my beloved and my friend.
As a sign of my love, I give you this ring.

BRIDE:

By the will of God and the desire of my heart, I take you,
Tom, as my husband to have and to hold from this day
forward. I love you and accept you as you are and as you will
become. I give you all that I am and all that I possess. And
by my willing submission to your headship, I will seek to
demonstrate the church's joyful submission to Christ, her
head.

As we walk together, I believe that whether God allows
riches or poverty, sickness or health, peace or persecution,
He will work everything for our good, as He promised. And
in all these things I will stand with you as we become more
than conquerors through Him who loves us.

Tom, I promise to continue my walk with God and to
develop the beauty of a gentle and quiet spirit. I will encourage you, pray for you, and always seek to be a helper to you.
I promise to work toward a growing communication, with-
holding nothing from you, and will learn with you as we
become heirs together of the grace of life.

Through the power of the Holy Spirit, my love for you will
be patient and kind, not jealous or boastful, arrogant or rude.
I will not insist on my own way, or be irritable or resentful.
I will keep no record of your wrongs, but will rejoice in the
truth. My love will always protect, always trust, always hope,
always endure.

Throughout our life together, you are my beloved and my
friend.

As a sign of my love, I give you this ring.

GROOM:

I, Glen, take you, Kathy, to be my wedded wife. With deepest joy I receive you into my life, that together we may be one. As Christ is to His body, the church, so I will be to you, a faithful and sacrificial husband. I promise you my deepest love, my unselfish devotion, and my tenderest care. I promise to direct our lives into a life of faith in Jesus Christ, honoring God's guidance by His Spirit through His Word. Therefore, Kathy, I pledge to you my life as a loving and faithful husband.

BRIDE:

I, Kathy, take you, Glen, to be my wedded husband. With deepest joy I receive you into my life, that together we may be one. With confidence I submit myself to your headship as unto the Lord, and I promise you my deepest love, my unselfish devotion, and my tenderest care. Because God has prepared me for you, I will ever strengthen, help, comfort, and encourage you. Therefore, Glen, I pledge to you my life as a loving and faithful wife.

GROOM/BRIDE:

By the choice of God and by the choice of my heart, I take thee, Viki/Ralph, to be the companion of my life and the object of my love. I pledge myself to you alone with a devotion that shall increase as we pass together through sorrow and joy, through darkness and sunlight, and through all the circumstances of life that God may send our way. I joyfully forsake all other claims to my affections, and with faith and tenderness promise to live with you, to love you, to cherish you, and to be separated from you only when God shall call one of us home to be with Him.

GROOM:

I vow these things to you before our heavenly Father, our families, and friends. My first love will always be our God and Father and the Lord Jesus Christ. He is my Head and Lord, and Him will I serve all the days of my life.

But you, my love, are the perfect gift from the hand of our Father. He has given you to me, to be my helpmeet, just as Eve was to Adam. She made him complete, just as you do me.

Paul said, "Love is patient, love is kind, is not jealous; love does not brag and is not arrogant; does not act unbecomingly; it does not seek its own, is not provoked, does not take into account a wrong suffered, does not rejoice in unrighteousness, but rejoices with the truth. Love bears all things, believes all things, hopes all things, endures all things. Love never fails."

This love I vow to you by the power of God's Spirit in my life.

Also Paul said I should love you just as Christ loved the church and gave Himself up for her. This, too, I vow to you: a love that always seeks your good to the glory of God, a love that gives up all my rights, to serve you.

Again Paul said that I am your head just as Christ is the Head of the church. I am your head to look only for your good, to lead and guide you, to protect you, to provide for you, to strengthen and encourage you, and most of all bring you closer to the heart of our heavenly Father.

This is my heart's desire, and my vow to you this day. I know that I will fall short of this kind of love, and only depending on God's grace can I even hope to love you in this way. Yet this is my heart's prayer for our marriage, and this is my vow.

BRIDE:

Steve, as we stand before our Lord, our families, and our friends, I vow to you my love and my devotion. My love for you is a commitment of my will that will not waver. All that I am is yours, and all that I have is yours.

I promise always to keep God first in my life, to love Him, and to worship Him. This is the only way I can be the wife you deserve. Only God can give me a selfless love which seeks your good above mine and desires nothing in return. This I pray will be true.

By the power of the Holy Spirit working in me, I vow to you a love which is patient, kind, not jealous, not boastful, and not proud. A love which is not rude, not self-seeking, not easily angered, and keeps no record of wrongs. My love will not delight in evil but will rejoice in truth. It will always protect, always trust, always hope, and always persevere. My love for you will never fail.

Steve, you are now my head as Christ is the Head of the church. I promise to follow your direction and your leadership. I vow to you my submission and my obedience. I will respect and honor you. I will strive to be teachable and of a quiet and gentle spirit.

As God created Eve for Adam, so I have been created to be a helper to you. I desire to meet your every need and to help you in every way. I promise to listen to you, encourage you, comfort you, and to stand by you always. I will strive to be sensitive to your needs and to meet them.

As we begin our life as one today, I gladly lay aside all my rights, to serve you. I cleave to you and pray God will make our life pleasing and glorifying to Him.

GROOM:

Madelle, I want to respond today before these people and before God by taking you as my wife. I promise faithfully to love, honor, respect, and protect you as long as we both shall live. I promise to share my inner thoughts with you and hide nothing from you. I promise to recognize the abilities, strengths, and gifts God has given you and encourage you to use them to His greatest possible glory.

Because of my permanent commitment to you, I promise to provide for you through riches or poverty, through sickness or health, or through whatever may come. I promise that both my commitment to God and to you, with the family that God may give us, will come before my commitment to my profession. I promise to seek and accept God's direction as I fill the role of leadership in our home.

I am giving you this ring today as a tangible symbol of these promises.

BRIDE:

John, in the presence of these people and in the presence of God here among us, I take you as my husband. And I promise to love you, to be faithfully committed to you, to share with you my inner being, my thoughts, and my private emotions. I will respect you and your God-given authority in our relationship and will follow your leadership as you follow Christ's.

You have been given many abilities and gifts. I promise to encourage you as you allow God to use them. I promise to give you freedom to develop both personally and professionally. I promise to provide a positive support for you and stand with you in the face of whatever may come, easy or hard, until death parts us, depending on God for strength.

I am giving you this ring today as a tangible symbol of these promises.

GROOM:

Shari, God has been faithfully building in us a growing love. The foundation of this love is not human affection alone, but a strong and abiding sense of God's calling.

Therefore, my beloved, I promise both you and our Father in heaven that I will strive to love you as Christ loved the church. I will serve you and consider you more important than myself.

I promise also to strive to walk worthy of God's calling. Only then will I be able to offer leadership and encouragement as we go on our adventure toward wholeness in Christ.

This I vow in the faith and hope instilled and nurtured in us by the Spirit of God.

BRIDE:

Jim, I believe God has called us to serve Him together. I believe my first priority is my own relationship to God, and, second, to you.

I want to encourage you, to stimulate you, to challenge you in your walk toward maturity in Christ.

My prayer is that our love may abound more and more in knowledge and depth of insight so that our relationship and our lives together may bring honor and glory to God.

GROOM:

Bonnie, I consider myself an exceedingly blessed man by all Jesus has given me in and through you. I love you, and I really believe in you as a woman, and I with much joy take the responsibility God has given me to meet your needs and to love you in the way that He designed me to. I want to allow you, Bonnie, to be free to be all that God meant you to be. I want to love you, care for you, give to you, trust you, and sacrifice for you in much the same way as Christ gave Himself a sacrifice for His bride, the church. I want to be an imitator of Jesus in everything I do and say, for it is only then that I can truly love you.

BRIDE:

Paul, I read in the Word that Jesus calls us to be His bride, and now I'm in the position of becoming your bride. Jesus calls us to recognize His authority and obey it, and I recognize you as an authority over me, for God has placed you there. I want to vow to you that I will respect you and build you up as a man, and will try to meet your needs as God helps me. I want you to share all your inner thoughts with me, and I want to be your friend. I want to grow with you. I want to laugh and cry with you. Most of all, Paul, I want to reach toward Jesus with you more and more every day. I love you, and I plan on loving you with all the love that God can give me.

GROOM/BRIDE:

I love you, Carol/Mike. Before our family and friends, and most importantly before our Lord, I take you to be my wife/husband and give to you all that I am and have.

Just as I have been loved unconditionally by Jesus Christ, so I promise to love you unconditionally. In the weakness of my love, I will rely on the strength of His love.

I vow that I will never purposefully hinder the Holy Spirit in our relationship. I will come to you with a vulnerable, teachable spirit, ready to respond to your nurturing love. I will communicate with you consistently, offering you honesty and respect. I will seek the constructive resolution of conflict between us, always looking out for your best interest. Just as God forgives me, so I will always forgive you.

GROOM'S VARIATION:

Carol, as head of our home I will lead you with the love that the Lord Jesus has shown to us. I will provide for you and protect you as God shall make me able.

BRIDE'S VARIATION:

Mike, as your wife I will strive to become a supportive, understanding, and godly wife, submitting to your loving leadership as unto Christ.

BOTH VOWS CONTINUED:

I will daily seek wisdom in ministering to your emotional, spiritual, physical, and intellectual needs. I will affirm you, encourage you, and edify you. I will always remain faithful to you.

Because Jesus Christ is the most important Person in our lives, I commit myself to helping you grow in the fullness and stature of Christ. It is only in Him we are made one. We will continue to seek His perfect will for our lives, serving Him and praising Him together.

I love you now and will love you as long as God shall give me life.

Other Phrases to Consider

I promise to love you in the everydayness of life.

I will allow you to differ with me.

I will honor your goals and dreams.

I will be honest with you, continuing to reveal myself totally to you.

I will learn to know you, so we can become closer and more deeply united as one in Christ.

I will keep our love growing and never let it fall in stagnant security.

In asking you to become a part of my life, I am fully conscious of the responsibilities I am assuming.

I will continue to maintain and strengthen the bond that draws me to you.

I dedicate myself to learning about your world—your needs and desires, your vulnerabilities and values, your likes and dislikes. I will be sensitive to your emotional and intellectual pleasures and encourage your spiritual growth.

I will resolve all barriers that may arise in our relationship and will not let the sun go down on any wrath.

I accept you for who you are, and will never ask you to give more than you are capable or willing to give. Yet I will encourage you to develop those valuable qualities and abilities I know are within you.

I will think of ways to brighten each day, and will not let a day pass without telling you of my love.

I promise not to focus on your negative qualities, but to focus on that which is true, honorable, right, pure, lovely, and of good repute.

. . . for as long as we both shall live or until Christ, who has saved us by His grace, returns to take us unto Himself forever.

My love is only the beginning of what it will become as I grow in the Lord and mature into the person you need me to be.

I love you because He first loved me.

Giving and Receiving of Rings

Some ministers explain the symbolism of the ring this way. Gold, the purest of metals, symbolizes the pureness of Christian marriage, and a circle symbolizes never-ending love. If this is done frequently at weddings in your area, you might wish to eliminate the explanation lest it become trite.

Some offer this prayer before the giving of each ring: "Bless, O Lord, this ring, that he/she who gives it and she/he who wears it may abide in your peace and continue in your favor until their life's end."

You may choose the wording with which you give the ring. Here are a few suggestions:

I give you this ring as a sign of my love—a love I will continue giving all our days.

This ring I give you in token and pledge of our constant faith and abiding love; in the name of the Father, and of the Son, and of the Holy Spirit. Amen.

I give you this ring as a symbol of my abiding love. I ask that you wear it, so that all may know we are one.

Giver: In token and in pledge of our constant faith and abiding love, with this ring I thee wed.

Receiver: May it keep you ever in my heart and mind when we are absent from each other.

I give you this ring as I give you my love.

22
Prayers for Your Marriage

Prayer usually follows the exchange of vows, and for good reason. Only God can give the strength and wisdom to keep such promises for a lifetime. As you bow, you acknowledge your dependence on him.

The couple may kneel, or simply bow their heads, as the minister leads a prayer for their marriage. Or the groom, as spiritual head of the home, could lead in prayer, followed by a pastoral prayer.

You might ask each member of the wedding party to offer a short prayer. Plan these beforehand so that each is succinct but meaningful.

The vocalist could sing a prayer song. The vocalist or the congregation might sing "The Lord's Prayer" or "Lord, Make Them an Instrument of Thy Peace." If you print the words in a program, you'll find that most people know the melody.

The congregation could pray the Lord's Prayer. Either provide printed words, or have the minister say whether he will use *debt* and *debtors* or *trespasses.*

Both bride and groom may pray (be sure to have a microphone if you are kneeling with your backs to the congregation). One couple used this prayer as their vow to God:

TOGETHER: Thank You, Father, for doing all things well. Your bringing us together is an example of this, and we do thank You.

GROOM: We've given You our lives individually, Lord. Now we want to reaffirm this commitment jointly.

BRIDE: We want to invite You to come live in our home, and we recognize Your right to rule us. Because we trust You, we can do this without fear.

GROOM: Just as we promise to love each other, we promise to love and be faithful to You. Make us an example of Your love to those around us.

BRIDE: We promise to spend regular time with You in Your Word, to pray for each other, and to encourage each other in Christian growth.

GROOM: As for the children You may give us, we promise to teach them of You and live a consistent example before them.

BRIDE: Lord, these have been big promises we've made to each other and to You today. We need Your help.

GROOM: You know that we've made promises in the past that we were unable to keep. And You know how weak we are.

TOGETHER: We seek Your strength. Live through us in a way we cannot live ourselves, and unite us as we submit to Your Lordship. Amen.

One couple used a printed prayer in their program for the congregation to read:

MEN: Dear Father, look with favor upon the world You have made, and for which Your Son gave His life, and especially upon this man and this woman whom You make one in holy matrimony.

WOMEN: Give them wisdom and devotion in the ordering of their common life, that each may be to the other a strength in need, a counselor in perplexity, a comfort in sorrow, and a companion in joy.

MEN: Grant that their wills may be so knit together in

Your will, and their spirits in Your Spirit, that they may grow in love and peace with You and each other all the days of their life.

WOMEN: Give them grace, when they hurt each other, to recognize and acknowledge their fault and to seek each other's forgiveness and Yours.

MEN: Make their life together a sign of Christ's love to this sinful and broken world, that unity may overcome estrangement, forgiveness heal guilt, and joy conquer despair.

WOMEN: Bestow on them, if it is Your will, the gift and heritage of children, and the grace to bring them up to know You, to love You, and to serve You.

MEN: Give them such fulfillment of their mutual affection that they may reach out in love and concern for others.

WOMEN: Grant that all married persons who have witnessed these vows may find their lives strengthened and their loyalties confirmed.

ALL: Grant that Your will may be done on earth as it is in heaven, where You, O Father, with Your Son and the Holy Spirit live and reign together, now and forever. Amen.

Another couple used this prayer based on the New International Version's translation of Ephesians 3:14–21 and printed it in their programs, for the congregation to read in unison:

For this reason we kneel before the Father from whom his whole family in heaven and on earth derives its name. We pray that out of his glorious riches he may strengthen you with power through his Spirit in your inner being, so that Christ may dwell in your hearts through faith. And we pray that you, being rooted and grounded in love, may have power together with all the saints, to grasp how wide and long and high and deep is the love of Christ, and to know this love that surpasses knowledge—that you may be filled to the measure of all the fullness of God.

Now to him who is able to do immeasurably more than all we ask or imagine, according to his power that is at work within us, to him be glory in the church and in Christ Jesus throughout all generations, for ever and ever! Amen.

You may also invite spontaneous prayers from the congregation.

Declaration of Marriage

The minister now makes the happy pronouncement that you are husband and wife (more appropriate wording than *man and wife*).

You may now seal your vows with a kiss. As one minister advises, make it more than a peck, but less than a passion. No doubt you'll get plenty of practice—but do practice! One couple both tilted their heads the same direction, bumping noses. Another had not quite decided whether she would put her arms around his neck or around his waist. So decide exactly how you will execute this kiss—and enjoy your practice!

At one wedding the minister invited, "Let's applaud as they seal their vows with a kiss." The couple felt this relieved the tension that built during the wedding.

At another wedding, guests had been given small bells which they rang during the kiss as an expression of their joy.

Covenants

Some couples, after their vows and after being pronounced husband and wife, make a mutual covenant. One couple made this covenant: "We will resolve all difficulties through prayer, communicating with God, and communicating with each other. We will never consider divorce as a solution to any problem."

Because we believed that marriage in Christ involves a way of life ordained in Scripture not only between ourselves, but also fellowship with other believers and witness to unbelievers, we read together this covenant of life:

> As we begin our life together, we covenant, God helping us, that we will love each other, pray for each other, and seek to help each other grow in grace and in the knowledge of our Lord Jesus Christ.
>
> We will put away from us all bitterness, wrath, anger, and evil speaking; and we will be kind to each other, tenderhearted, forgiving each other even as God for Christ's sake has forgiven us.
>
> We will not forsake assembling with other believers for worship and service, but will honor the Word of God and will seek to follow those who have the spiritual rule over us. We will be good stewards of all that God has given us, and will give as God has prospered us.
>
> We will seek to win others to Christ by sharing the Gospel in word and deed. As we have opportunity, we will do good to all men, especially those who are of the household of faith. We will strive to carry out His commission to spread the Gospel throughout the whole world.

Candle Ceremony

Many couples use a three-candle ceremony to symbolize their lives blending into one. Each takes a candle (already lit), and together they light a center candle. Some then blow out the candles representing their individual lives. However, it seems more appropriate to leave these burning because marriage does not snuff out your individuality.

One couple had two girls, dressed as bridesmaids, lead their processional holding lit candles. The girls then sat in the choir loft throughout the ceremony, and handed the candles to the bride and groom. Together they lit a large pillar candle, now used for their anniversaries.

Another couple had their mothers come and give them the lit candles, symbolizing their giving of life.

Another chose to symbolize the union of two unique persons being united to one another and to Christ. Using a long white taper to symbolize Christ in His holiness, they molded a yellow and a green candle around the white one. The bride used a yellow candle (symbolizing the radiance of Christ's love) and the groom a green (symbolizing the growth of their lives in Him) to light the twisted triple taper. "Together," their program explained, "these candles express the goal of our union: to grow in Christ and radiate His love to all whose lives we touch."

Some couples have given each guest (excluding children) a small candle in a paper-plate holder. At the candle-lighting ceremony, ushers light the candles of the guests seated at the ends of the pews. They in turn then light the candles of the next guest, and so on, to symbolize everyone's commitment to help keep the flame of love glowing.

Benediction

You may have the congregation sing a benediction from the back of your hymnal or a selection such as "May the Grace of Christ Our Saviour."

Or the pastor may give the benediction. Here are several suggestions:

> The Lord bless you and keep you; the Lord make His face to shine upon you and be gracious unto you; the Lord lift up His countenance upon you and give you peace, both now and in the life everlasting. Amen.

> For I am confident of this very thing, that He who began a good work in you will perfect it until the day of Christ Jesus.
>
> Philippians 1:6 NAS

> Now the God of peace, who brought up from the dead the great Shepherd of the sheep through the blood of the eternal covenant, even Jesus our Lord, equip you in every good thing to do His will, working in us that which is pleasing in His sight, through Jesus Christ, to whom be the glory forever and ever. Amen.
>
> Hebrews 13:20, 21 NAS

> Now may goodness and mercy follow you all the days of your lives until you dwell in the house of the Lord forever. Amen.

Recessional

Select joyous, triumphant music either for instruments or for the congregation to sing. When this point comes, you can't help but smile with joy and relief! After the maid of honor straightens your train and hands you your bouquet, you will march out, happily wed. You may wish to stop and give a kiss to your parents. Or link arms with your parents and all exit together.

The pastor makes any announcements after the bridal party has left. He may instruct the congregation to remain seated until ushers dismiss by rows to go to the receiving line. If you are having no receiving line, he may announce, "Please go directly to the reception, where Mark and Mary will greet you personally." Or he may invite them to remain seated to watch the picture taking.

23
Three Innovative Weddings

Jim and Shari wanted a wedding that would glorify God and express God's creativity. They chose as their wedding theme, "Come, let us exalt His name together" with a logo of uplifted hands which a friend designed. They had this theme and logo on their invitations, on a banner over the guest book, on their programs, and on a batik which friends gave to hang at the front of the sanctuary.

They planned a worship service of Scripture and hymns to "exalt His name." After the processional and welcome by the pastor, four brothers-in-law formed a readers' theater, with three sections of choral readings, each leading to a hymn. Some lines they said in unison, some solo, and some duet. Their program follows:

> *God as Creator:* Psalms 95:6; Psalms 24:1, 2; Colossians 1:16, 17; Psalms 95:4–6; and Psalms 95:7
>
> Congregation: "All Creatures of Our God and King," Assisi
>
> *God as King:* Psalms 45:1–3; Psalms 24:8–10; Psalms 95:1–3; and Psalms 29:10
>
> Congregation: "Praise My Soul, the King of Heaven," Lyte
>
> *God as Lover:* Psalms 63:3, 4; Psalms 89:1; Psalms 117:2; Psalms 85:10; Psalms 107:15; 1 John 4:7–9; John 3:16; 1 John 4:11, 19.
>
> Vocalist: "Wedding Song," Paul Stookey

During this solo, the bridal party took their places on the platform. After a brother explained marriage from Genesis, each parent gave a four-minute counsel.

Jim and Shari then gave their vows from memory and exchanged rings.

For their candle-lighting ceremony, they had molded three tapers into one. "Marriage is not a solo or a duet, but a trio with God," they explained.

Then, while Jim and Shari knelt, their two honor attendants, their pastor, and two people who had contributed significantly to their spiritual growth laid hands on them and commited their marriage to God.

They marched out joyously to Handel's "Hallelujah Chorus."

After a simple cake-and-punch reception at church, they had a buffet at home to visit more intimately with family and out-of-town guests. Here they opened their wedding gifts so the family could join in their joy. By beginning the wedding in the early afternoon, they were still able to leave for their honeymoon in the early evening.

Paul and Bonnie wanted to exalt God's view of marriage and to demonstrate their love and continuity with their families. Although they expected about four hundred guests, they wanted an informal atmosphere.

They set the tone with a classical guitar prelude. Their service began when a friend stood in the balcony and read Jeremiah 33:11, "The voice of joy, and the voice of gladness, the voice of the bridegroom, and the voice of the bride, the voice of them that shall say, Praise the Lord of hosts: for the Lord is good; for his mercy endureth for ever. . . ."

The congregation then sang "Praise Ye the Lord, the Almighty." The pastor read Genesis 2:4–7, the creation of man, after which Paul walked down the aisle between his parents, followed by his brothers and sister. Then the pastor read Genesis 2:18–22, the creation of woman, as Bonnie's family walked down the aisle, Bonnie walking between her eldest brother and mother.

When they reached the front of the sanctuary, the pastor read Genesis 2:24, the first marriage.

To dramatize this Scripture, Paul and Bonnie planned a "leave taking" ceremony. Each family formed a diagonal line, facing both each other and the congregation. Paul then took two steps out, and turned to speak directly to his family.

He said, "Dad and Mom, I really love both of you and thank God for you. It is because of you that I can stand before God and before my brothers and sisters here today. I am a happy man because you cared for me as a whole person, physically, mentally, and above all else, spiritually. And both of you took time out of your lives to develop my spirit. So I thank you for your love, for your instructions, and for living before me an example of loving Christ, which has made your love so beautiful."

His father then responded, "Paul, as you go from us to be joined to Bonnie, you have Mom's and my blessing and our prayer that your experience in marriage will be happy and loving as you saw ours was. May yours be even more."

Bonnie then took two steps out and turned to speak to her family. "I, too, want to express my love to my family before my friends and relatives and most of all before my Lord God. I thank my brothers Bob and Jim for upholding me as I follow God's teaching. I thank you for finding two wonderful sisters-in-law. Sue and Gail, you have become true sisters to me. Most of all, I thank my mother for being my best friend. I thank you for your love and true concern for me."

Because her father was deceased, her elder brother responded for the family, "Bonnie, we love you, and now give you to be joined to Paul."

The mothers then were seated in the congregation, and

Paul's father, a minister, joined the pastor to conduct the remainder of the service.

After a brother sang, a close friend in the congregation stood and prayed. Paul's father then counseled the couple about their marriage.

After a more traditional section with music, vows, prayer, and exchange of rings, Paul and Bonnie were declared husband and wife. The pastor invited the congregation to express their joy by clapping as the couple kissed. The pastor prayed, then all recited the Lord's Prayer.

"Paul and Bonnie will now share their first meal together," the pastor said. So while the congregation sang, "We Are One in the Spirit," the new couple was served communion.

Volunteers were then invited to come, lay hands on the couple, and pray. As more and more came, they formed a semicircle. No longer able to lay hands on the couple, they laid hands on the shoulder of the guest standing in front of them. Then everyone quietly sang "Alleluia" as the guests returned to their seats.

To keep the informal feeling, Paul and Bonnie publicly thanked their guests for making their wedding so beautiful before they marched out to the recessional.

Dave and Debbie solved the frustration of too little time to visit with family and out-of-town guests by having a weekend-long wedding. Because both came from missionary families, they had guests coming from all over the world.

Because so many of their friends had become cynical about marriage, Dave and Debbie wanted their prolonged celebration and hour-and-a-half ceremony to exalt God's ideal and affirm that marriage is a beautiful covenant to be entered joyfully.

Dave and Debbie rented part of their church camp for a wedding retreat. Younger guests stayed in tents, while older adults enjoyed the comforts of a lodge. Most meals were cooked outdoors.

Guests arrived Thursday evening for dinner, followed by recreation and get-acquainted activities, then a campfire.

Friday after free time and lunch, Debbie's father led a group Bible study on the meaning of marriage. That afternoon, as the wedding party rehearsed, those not involved helped with the rehearsal dinner.

After dinner Dave and Debbie allowed a time for giving. They had asked each guest to share something of themselves rather than purchase presents. Those who wished publicly presented their gifts: songs, poems, readings, paintings, an embroidered picture, a wood carving, and more.

Saturday morning several friends conducted a worship service, then dedicated the nuptial couple. A communion service followed, in which Dave and Debbie served each guest—their way to express their love. After a light love feast/lunch, it was time to prepare for the wedding.

They chose "Alleluia" as their theme. A calligrapher hand-lettered their invitation to the retreat, their wedding invitations, and their programs, all with the "Alleluia" theme.

Their wedding took place by the lake. The only decoration besides the trees and hills was an arch that friends had made and covered with greens.

As guests arrived, ushers handed each a program and a daisy, which they could add to the arch, symbolizing that each had added beauty to Dave's and Debbie's lives.

Music was provided by three guitarists and a flute. A vocalist sang "All Good Gifts" from *Godspell* for the processional, with the wedding party singing the final verse as the bridal couple came over a small hill. The attendants then sat in a semicircle of chairs, with the bridal couple sitting in the center, facing the congregation. The minister stood under the arch.

The attendants led the worship with a wedding liturgy. They had rehearsed a choral reading of verses showing God's love through creation, through the church, and through marriage. Through this recital of Scripture, Dave and Debbie wanted to communicate that marriage is ordained by God and given as an expression of His love.

Following a solo, the parents each gave counsel to the couple. Then Dave and Debbie exchanged vows and rings, and had the maid of honor and best man offer prayers. The vocalist sang "Be Still and Know That I Am God" as a response.

The congregation sang "Joyful, Joyful, We Adore Thee" as a recessional.

24
The Traditional
Wedding Service

At the day and time appointed for Solemnization of
Matrimony, the Persons to be married shall come into
the body of the Church, or shall be ready in some proper
house, with their friends and neighbours; and there
standing together, the Man on the right hand, and the
Woman on the left, the Minister shall say,

Dearly beloved, we are gathered together here in the
sight of God, and in the face of this company, to join together
this Man and this Woman in holy Matrimony; which is an
honourable estate, instituted by God, signifying unto us the
mystical union that is betwixt Christ and his Church: which
holy estate Christ adorned and beautified with his presence
and first miracle that he wrought in Cana of Galilee, and is
commended of Saint Paul to be honourable among all men:
and therefore is not by any to be entered into unadvisedly
or lightly; but reverently, discreetly, advisedly, soberly, and
in the fear of God. Into this holy estate these two persons
present come now to be joined. If any man can show just
cause, why they may not lawfully be joined together, let him
now speak, or else hereafter for ever hold his peace.

And also speaking unto the Persons who are to be married,
he shall say,

I require and charge you both, as ye will answer at the

dreadful day of judgment when the secrets of all hearts shall
be disclosed, that if either of you know any impediment,
why ye may not be lawfully joined together in Matrimony,
ye do now confess it. For be ye well assured, that if any
persons are joined together otherwise than as God's Word
doth allow, their marriage is not lawful.

*. . . if no impediment is alleged, or suspected, the Minister
shall say to the Man,*

_____, wilt thou have this Woman to thy wedded wife, to
live together after God's ordinance in the holy estate of
Matrimony? Wilt thou love her, comfort her, honour, and
keep her in sickness and in health; and, forsaking all others,
keep thee only unto her, so long as ye both shall live?

The Man shall answer,

I will.

Then shall the Minister say unto the Woman,

_____, wilt thou have this Man to thy wedded husband,
to live together after God's ordinance in the holy estate of
Matrimony? Wilt thou love him, comfort him, honour, and
keep him in sickness and in health; and, forsaking all others,
keep thee only unto him, so long as ye both shall live?

The Woman shall answer,

I will.

Then shall the Minister say,

Who giveth this Woman to be married to this Man?

*. . . The Minister, receiving the Woman at her father's or
friend's hands, shall cause the Man with his right hand to
take the Woman by her right hand, and to say after him as
followeth.*

I, _____, take thee, _____, to be my wedded Wife, to
have and to hold from this day forward, for better for worse,
for richer for poorer, in sickness and in health, to love and
to cherish, till death us do part, according to God's holy
ordinance; and thereto I plight thee my troth.

Then shall they loose their hands; and the Woman with

her right hand taking the Man by his right hand, shall like-wise say after the Minister,

I, _____, take thee, _____, to my wedded Husband, to have and to hold from this day forward, for better for worse, for richer for poorer, in sickness and in health, to love and to cherish, till death us do part, according to God's holy ordinance; and thereto I give thee my troth.

Then shall they again loose their hands; and the Man shall give unto the Woman a Ring on this wise: the Minister taking the Ring shall deliver it unto the Man, to put it upon the fourth finger of the Woman's left hand. And the Man holding the Ring there, and taught by the Minister, shall say,

With this ring I thee wed: In the Name of the Father, and of the Son, and of the Holy Ghost. Amen.

And before delivering the Ring to the Man, the Minister may say as followeth.

Bless, O Lord, this Ring, that he who gives it and she who wears it may abide in thy peace, and continue in thy favour, unto their life's end; through Jesus Christ our Lord. Amen.

Then, the Man leaving the Ring upon the fourth finger of the Woman's left hand, the Minister shall say,

Let us pray.

Then shall the Minister and the People, still standing, say the Lord's Prayer.

Our Father, who art in heaven, Hallowed be thy Name. Thy kingdom come. Thy will be done, On earth as it is in heaven. Give us this day our daily bread. And forgive us our trespasses, As we forgive those who trespass against us. And lead us not into temptation, But deliver us from evil. For thine is the kingdom, and the power, and the glory, for ever and ever. Amen.

Then shall the Minister add:

O eternal God, Creator and Preserver of all mankind, Giver of all spiritual grace, the Author of everlasting life;

Send thy blessing upon these thy servants, this man and this woman, whom we bless in thy Name; that they, living faithfully together, may surely perform and keep the vow and covenant betwixt them made, (whereof this Ring given and received is a token and pledge,) and may ever remain in perfect love and peace together, and live according to thy laws; through Jesus Christ our Lord. *Amen.*

The Minister may add one or both of the following prayers.

O Almighty God, Creator of mankind, who only art the well-spring of life; Bestow upon these thy servants, if it be thy will, the gift and heritage of children; and grant that they may see their children brought up in thy faith and fear, to the honour and glory of thy Name; through Jesus Christ our Lord. *Amen.*

O God, who hast so consecrated the state of Matrimony that in it is represented the spiritual marriage and unity betwixt Christ and his Church; Look mercifully upon these thy servants, that they may love, honour, and cherish each other, and so live together in faithfulness and patience, in wisdom and true godliness, that their home may be a haven of blessing and of peace; through the same Jesus Christ our Lord, who liveth and reigneth with thee and the Holy Spirit ever, one God, world without end. *Amen.*

Then shall the Minister join their right hands together, and say,

Those whom God hath joined together let no man put asunder.

Then shall the Minister speak unto the company.

Forasmuch as _____ and _____ have consented together in holy wedlock, and have witnessed the same before God and this company, and thereto have given and pledged their troth, each to the other, and have declared the same by giving and receiving a Ring, and by joining hands; I pronounce that they are Man and Wife, In the Name of the

Father, and of the Son, and of the Holy Ghost. Amen.

The Man and Wife kneeling, the Minister shall add this Blessing.

God the Father, God the Son, God the Holy Ghost, bless, preserve, and keep you; the Lord mercifully with his favour look upon you, and so fill you with all spiritual benediction and grace; that ye may so live together in this life, that in the world to come ye may have life everlasting. *Amen.*

25
A Contemporary Marriage Service

Before the date and time of the marriage have been announced, the pastor will have counseled with the couple to be married about the nature of marriage and the order of the marriage service.

It is appropriate to publish the announcement of the wedding in the church bulletin prior to the service in a form such as this:

_____ and _____ have announced their intention to be joined in marriage on _____. They ask for your prayers that they may enter into this union in the name of the Lord and be prospered in it.

A printed wedding folder containing the order of service helps to establish the theme of the service through such elements as the reading of the Scriptures, the proclamation of the Word, hymns, and the music. . . .

The wedding party may enter either during the processional music or during the singing of a congregational hymn. The woman will stand on the minister's right and the man on the left, with the other members of the wedding party on either side.

Address to the People

We, as a community of friends, are gathered here in God's presence, to witness the marriage of _____ and _____, and to ask God to bless them.

We are called to rejoice in their happiness, to help them when they have trouble, and to remember them in our prayers. Marriage, like our creation as men and women, owes its existence to God. It is his will and purpose that a husband and wife should love each other throughout their life (and that children born to them should enjoy the security of family and home).

Prayer

When the marriage rite is not part of a full worship service, the minister may pray:

Eternal God, our Creator and Redeemer, as you gladdened the wedding at Cana in Galilee by the presence of your Son, so by your presence now bring your joy to this wedding. In favor look upon this couple and grant that they, rejoicing in all your gifts, may at length celebrate with Christ the Bridegroom, the marriage feast which has no end. Amen.

Charge to Couple

Speaking to the persons being married, the minister shall say:

_____ and _____, your marriage is intended to join you for life in a relationship so intimate and personal that it will change your whole being. God offers you the hope, and indeed the promise, of a love that is true and mature.

You have made it known that you want to be joined in Christian marriage, and no one has shown any valid reason why you may not. If either of you knows of any reason, you are now to declare it.

Declaration of Consent

Speaking to the groom, the minister will say:

_____, do you take _____ to be your wife, and do you commit yourself to her, to be responsible in the marriage relationship, to give yourself to her in love and work, to invite her fully into your being so that she can know who you are, to cherish her above all others and to respect her individuality, encouraging her to be herself and to grow in all that God intends?

The groom will answer:

Yes, I will.

Speaking to the bride, the minister will say:

_____, do you take _____ to be your husband, and do you commit yourself to him, to be responsible in the marriage relationship, to give yourself to him in love and work, to invite him fully into your being so that he can know who you are, to cherish him above all others and to respect his individuality, encouraging him to be himself and to grow in all that God intends?

The bride will answer:

Yes, I will.

Affirmation by Parents and Congregation

Inviting the parents to stand, the minister shall ask:

Do you as parents promise to pray for and support your children in this new relationship which they enter as husband and wife? If so, each say "I will."

I will.

Addressing the congregation, the minister will say:

All of you who witness these vows, will you do everything in your power to support and uphold these two persons in their marriage? Then say "We will!"

At this point, where space permits, the bride and groom and their two immediate attendants may move into the chancel.

Vows

The couple, taking each other's hands, shall say their vows:

I take you, ———, to be my wife from this day forward, to join with you and share all that is to come, and with the help of God, I promise to be faithful to you as he gives us life together.

I take you, ———, to be my husband from this day forward, to join with you and share all that is to come, and with the help of God, I promise to be faithful to you as he gives us life together.

Or:

I take you, ———, to be my wife. I promise before God and these witnesses to be your faithful husband, to share with you in plenty and in want, in joy and in sorrow, in sickness and in health, to forgive and strengthen you and to join with you so that together we may serve God and others as long as we both shall live.

I take you, ———, to be my husband. I promise before God and these witnesses to be your faithful wife, to share with you in plenty and in want, in joy and in sorrow, in sickness and in health, to forgive and strengthen you and to join with you so that together we may serve God and others as long as we both shall live.

Giving and Receiving of Rings

As the minister receives each ring in turn, it is appropriate to pray:

Bless, Lord, this ring that *he/she* who gives it and *she/he* who wears it may abide in your peace. Amen.

Giving the rings in turn, each shall say:

———, I love you, and I give you this ring as a sign of my love and faithfulness.

Declaration of Marriage

Because ——— and ——— have made their vows with each other before God and all of us here, I declare them to be husband and wife in the name of God: Father, Son, and Holy Spirit. Amen.

Let no one divide those whom God has united.

Blessing

The Lord God who created our first parents and established them in marriage, establish and sustain you, that you may find delight in each other and grow in holy love until life's end. Amen.

Prayers of Thanksgiving and Intercession

O God, Creator and Father of us all, we thank you for the gift of life—and, in life, for the gift of marriage. We praise and thank you for all the joys that can come to men and women through marriage, and for the blessings of home and family.

Today, especially, we think of ——— and ——— as they begin their life together as husband and wife. With them we thank you for the joy they find in each other. (We pray for their parents, that at this moment of parting they may rejoice in their children's happiness.) Give them strength, Father, to keep the vows they have made and cherish the love they share, that they may be faithful and devoted. Help them to support each other with patience, understanding, and honesty. (Teach them to be wise and loving parents of any children they may have.)

Look with favor, God, on all our homes. Defend them from every evil that may threaten them, from outside or within. Let your Spirit so direct all of us that we may each look to the good of others in word and deed and grow in grace as we advance in years; through Jesus Christ our Lord. Amen.

Here the Lord's Prayer may be included:

Lord's Prayer

Our Father who art in heaven,
   hallowed be thy Name,
   thy kingdom come,
   thy will be done,
     on earth as it is in heaven.
Give us this day our daily bread.
And forgive us our debts
   as we forgive our debtors.
And lead us not into temptation,
   but deliver us from evil.
For thine is the kingdom, and
  the power,
   and the glory forever. Amen.

Our Father in heaven,
   hallowed be your Name,
   your kingdom come,
   your will be done,
     on earth as in heaven.
Give us today our daily bread.
Forgive us our sins
   as we forgive those who sin against us.
Save us from the time of trial
   and deliver us from evil.
For the kingdom, the power, and
  the glory
   are yours now and forever. Amen.

Benediction

The Lord bless you and keep you; the Lord make his face to shine upon you, and be gracious to you; the Lord lift up his countenance upon you, and give you peace. Amen.

Or:

Almighty God, Father, Son, and Holy Spirit, direct and keep you in his light and truth and love all the days of your life. Amen.

Following the service, the wedding party may leave the church during a hymn, suitable instrumental music, or in silence.

26
The Reception

Your wedding service will be solemn and sacred. Your reception, however, gives time for festivity and celebration. So plan a party that you will truly enjoy.

Reception costs can vary widely from a catered sit-down dinner to cake and punch in the church fellowship hall. Your budget might limit the embellishments, but it need not limit the joyousness of the celebration. Before planning the details of your reception, think through both your values and your budget.

Which is more important to you—simple refreshments served to a large gathering of friends and relatives, or a meal served to a more limited guest list? Do you prefer to hire someone to do the work, or do you and a few friends have the time and energy to do it yourselves? Although this option will save costs, it might be physically draining. Even if you are an adept hostess, you will be under pressure for many other wedding details. And the reception calls for last-minute work. Some brides have made sandwiches and mixed punch, then found themselves too tired to truly enjoy their guests. So budget your energy as well as your money.

Many caterers specialize in wedding receptions and can handle all the details from decorating to serving the food to cleaning up afterward. Choose your caterer carefully, preferably on the recommendation of a friend. And get all estimates in writing.

Some caterers will allow you to provide some of the food or decorations, thus cutting the costs. You might consider this type of arrangement, providing food that can be prepared ahead, such as a salad bar with cold meats or a buffet of cheeses and cheese spreads accompanied with assorted crackers and vegetables. The caterer then handles all the set up, serving, and cleanup.

Budget Trimmer: Do you have capable friends who would handle the reception? If you know a good organizer who has experience in serving larger groups, consider hiring her. Give her detailed plans of what you would like served, the number of guests, type of decorations wanted, and estimated costs. Let her hire one or two others to help with the kitchen preparations and cleanup.

If you enjoy informality, you might plan a home or garden reception, or a backyard picnic or barbecue.

If the wedding and reception seem too much for one day, plan a reception a few weeks after your honeymoon. However you choose to celebrate the occasion, you should be happy and at ease.

Whatever your choice for a reception, you'll want to plan some or all of the following:

The receiving line: This custom provides an easy way to insure that everyone gets to greet the new bride and groom —and that you get to see each guest. You can form the receiving line immediately after the wedding, greeting guests as they exit. Or you can form the line at the entry to your reception. Some brides prefer to form a short receiving line as the first guests prepare to leave the reception. This allows for more leisurely conversation.

The receiving line can be as long or short as you wish. Either or both fathers may receive, if they like. The maid of honor and bridesmaids are usually included, standing in the order in which they walked in the processional. Although the best man and ushers are usually not included, you may wish to have them in the line if they would enjoy greeting the guests. Child attendants should not be required to stand in the line as they become restless.

The receiving line is usually formed in this order: mother of the bride, father of the groom (optional), mother of the groom, father of the bride (optional), the bride, the groom, the maid of honor, and bridesmaids.

All members of the receiving line stand in place until every guest has been greeted. At a large wedding this may take a half hour or more. Keep smiling, and try to be as cordial with the last guests as you were with the first.

Family circumstances may require some adjustments in the standard line. If your mother is not living, your father stands at the beginning of the line.

If your parents are divorced, your mother stands alone in the receiving line if she is giving the reception. Your father attends as a guest. If your father is giving the reception, he stands first in line, (unless he chooses to relinquish his place to the bride's mother) and the mother attends as a guest.

If either divorced parent has remarried, the spouse may act as host or hostess, but should not stand in line. If the groom's parents are divorced, only his mother stands in the line.

The cake: Whether or not you serve other food, you'll want a wedding cake. This may be home baked, bought at a bakery, or furnished by a caterer. If you buy the cake, call not only for estimates, but also ask that the cake be baked the morning of the wedding.

Although the wedding cake is traditionally white, it need not be white inside. Ask for your favorite: spice, chocolate, strawberry, whatever. Or order a different flavor for each layer.

Most bakeries have an assortment of decorations for the cake top, or can top it with fresh flowers. If you wish a top decoration with Christian symbolism, look in your Christian bookstore, then give the decoration to the bakery when you place your order.

Budget trimmer: Want a fancy cake for the pictures? Order a small one from the bakery. (Cut costs even further by having the top decorated with frosting roses at no extra charge.) Then have friends bake sheet cakes to arrange on the cake table. Carrot cakes or fruit cakes work especially well, since they can be baked ahead.

Cutting the cake: Traditionally the bride and groom cut the cake together, his right hand over hers, as a symbol of their new unity. Guests often expect to see you feed each other the first bites. Avoid any temptation to relieve tension by smearing frosting or other antics.

Wedding mementos: You might want to have napkins printed with your name and wedding date, or small photos of the bride for guests to remember your wedding. If your budget is limited, however, you can easily eliminate these items. Plain napkins will do the job.

Guest book: You'll want to remember the friends who honored you by attending your wedding. Most brides have a guest book for signatures. You might have this for guests to sign before they enter the wedding, or at the end of your receiving line. Or you could have a friend circulate the book at the reception, collecting the signatures. You may buy one of these books (often part of a larger memory book) at a stationery or department store. Or you (or an artistic friend) might make your own.

Music: A small orchestra or a pianist might be asked to play current love songs or old favorites. Or ask your soloist to sing some of your favorites.

Other entertainment: Some couples enjoy a short program. Have someone act as master of ceremonies, inviting the bride and groom to tell about their first meeting and future plans. Invite the parents and friends to give insights about the nuptial couple or to extend their best wishes.

You might want to make a photo display for the reception room with pictures from both of your childhood albums, snapshots of the two of you during courtship, and any formal portraits. Add any amusing memorabilia your guests might enjoy. Use your ingenuity to plan whatever entertainment that would make your day joyous and memorable.

Tossing the bouquet: Toward the end of the reception, after visiting with your guests, you may follow tradition by throwing your bouquet. The master of ceremonies or your maid of honor announces your plans and gathers all the unmarried girls. Superstition has it that the girl who catches the bouquet will become the next bride. If you wish to keep your bouquet, or if you are an older bride, you might not want to follow this custom.

Tossing the garter: After the bride throws her bouquet, the groom may remove her garter (discreetly worn below the knee) and toss it to the assembled single men. Same superstition—he's next to marry.

Saying good-bye: After the bouquet has been tossed, or the couple has finished greeting their guests, the bride and maid of honor go to change clothes. If the groom is formally dressed, he also goes to change. The best man should alert both sets of parents.

When you are both ready to go, take a few moments to give your thanks and good-byes to your parents. After hugs and kisses, run for the get-away car—perhaps showered by rice or confetti. (Be sure someone is assigned cleanup.)

27
Your Honeymoon

If visions of sugarplums dance in the heads of young children at Christmas, just as surely visions of a honeymoon dance in the heads of every engaged couple. No doubt you have dreams of intimacy—and ecstasy! Your honeymoon can be one of the most exquisite times of your life. Allow yourselves as much time as possible, for never again will you enjoy such carefree abandonment.

Honeymoons, however, can be less than idyllic. A bit of wise planning can make the difference between a dream trip and a nightmare. You don't think of anything going sour, but disappointments can occur. Wise is the couple who is prepared.

Before our marriage several recently married friends shared tidbits of what made their honeymoons happy—or what brought tears. We took advantage of their wisdom and gained a much more satisfying honeymoon.

The advice given here is the pooled wisdom of many honeymooners. Use it as a starter—then talk with the experts, your married friends. Nobody, of course, will share intimate details (nor will you). But most enjoy remembering that special trip and are glad to share what mistakes and good decisions they made.

Preparation for your honeymoon begins the week of your wedding. Plan wisely so that you don't run full-steam ahead all week. If, despite all your planning, you find a mile-long

174 Your Christian Wedding

list of jobs to be completed, ask friends for help. They'll be honored. Cut out all inconsequentials. You don't *have* to sew skirts for all the reception tables or make all the finger sandwiches. Better to skip a few niceties than to spoil your honeymoon. By making this decision, you'll be establishing a good priority: *you*, my love, are more important to me than anything else.

Pray specifically about your honeymoon. The God who inspired the Song of Solomon desires to give delight in marriage. He invites, "You may ask me for anything in my name, and I will do it" (John 14:14 NIV). So add your honeymoon to your prayer requests.

Your Wedding Night

Discuss your wedding night in detail, so that each knows what the other expects. Talk through any fears or inhibitions you may have. Even though you love each other deeply, it is normal to feel some anxiety about this venture into total love.

Prepare further by discussing together a book on sexual techniques. Even if you think you know everything and feel foolish reviewing basic biology, do it anyhow. *Intended for Pleasure* by Ed Wheat, M.D. and Gaye Wheat is thorough and helpful. By learning to talk specifically about sex, you'll lay a good foundation for talking after your marriage. Believe it or not, many couples find it difficult to verbalize their sexual pleasures or displeasures. Your intimate life will be much richer if you have learned to talk together.

When you arrive at your hotel, rest for a short while to allow the excitement of your wedding to ebb. Then go out for a quiet meal or light snack. Your eating probably has been irregular, and you may still think you are too excited to eat. But you'll need your energy sustained.

Honor God in your marriage by having a short devotional

time together. Share a favorite Scripture, then pray, thanking God for your union and asking His blessing on your new marriage.

Whether or not you proceed with your first sexual experience is your decision. Be prepared to be considerate, however, if either is exhausted.

Don't expect too much of your first experience. It will be special, and always a treasured memory. But sex is both a physical skill and a learned response. Your joy will increase from this day forward. But you probably won't have a perfect experience on your first attempt.

If you've learned any physical skill as an adult, keep the comparison in mind. The summer before our wedding I learned to ice skate. My first lesson I felt tense, and I certainly didn't perform graceful jumps and spins. Yet I was excited to be moving with skates on my feet. As the lessons progressed, I enjoyed each session a little more. I'd watch the more advanced skaters, anticipating the fun of spirals and spins.

Sex is much the same. Your first experience will be joyous just because you are free at last to express your love completely. But don't expect to reach a seventh heaven of ecstasy. This comes only with time and experience. Instead, be considerate and appreciative of the other's attempts. This, after all, is the foundation of true love.

Plan to Relax

Plan a relaxing trip. If you want to see Yellowstone, the Grand Tetons, the Redwood Forest, Disneyland, and the Grand Canyon, fine. Plan that trip a year from now when you'll enjoy it. Your honeymoon is not the time for a grand sight-seeing tour. Your biggest delight will come from enjoying each other. Plan a trip that offers enough enjoyable activities, but nothing so beckoning with tourist attractions that you feel compelled to rush from one to the other.

Unless you are both expert campers and hooked on the outdoors, this is probably not the time for a camping trip. You'll want to be clean, attractive, and comfortable—hard to manage while tenting. Find a cabin in the woods, if you like, with an occasional night spent under the stars.

Make all reservations early, then confirm them before you leave. One couple who failed to confirm arrived late for their wedding night, only to discover the hotel booked. It took an hour's drive to locate another room. By that time they were tense and exhausted.

Wherever you go for your honeymoon, stay within a fifty-mile radius of home for your wedding night. The wedding day is full enough without adding a long drive. Couples who attempted too much report bickering over petty issues, a result of needless exhaustion.

Try not to drive long distances on your honeymoon. Five hours is about the most you should schedule any day. One couple tackled a nine-hour drive their second day. The groom did all the driving. When they arrived at the motel, he was exhausted. The bride took her time getting pretty. As she stepped into the room ready to sweep him off his feet, she discovered her new husband sleeping fully clothed. She interpreted this to mean he no longer loved or desired her. In her anger, she curled on the couch to sleep. He awoke in the night wondering where he was—then discovered his bride. After some anger and tears they reached an understanding. But he recommends short drives to save such friction.

Be prepared to sleep much of your first week together. Usually you plan vacations filled with fun. But slow your pace for this one. You won't realize how much tension builds during prewedding days until you finally relax. The honeymoon with its adjustments also adds stress. So you'll probably find yourselves needing much more sleep than usual. The need for longer sleep might strike each of you at different times. So be prepared with a few solitary activities and large doses of understanding.

Plan your honeymoon budget carefully, but not tightly. Allow some fun money for each to blow. Or set aside an amount to purchase a whim. One couple received a cash gift with the instructions, "Spend it all on your honeymoon." With it they enjoyed several extravagances. Even if no one gives you such a gift, why not give it to yourselves?

Plan a few surprises. Bring along his favorite home-baked cookies. Have candles for romantic evenings. Hide a love note under his pillow. I packed two water pistols to start a playful fight. Begin a crazy game of "got you last." Use your imagination to think of ways to make your honeymoon fun.

Be prepared for some disappointments. Not everything will go exactly as planned. The weather could turn lousy. Have some puzzles and games in case it does.

Above all, be kind and considerate to each other. If your groom plans an activity that flops, appreciate his attempt rather than criticizing. Be always ready to communicate your feelings of disappointment as well as your joys. And be ready to forgive, for you'll discover that you each hurt and offend. Remember that you are learners, so don't expect perfection.

Lower your expectations, if you can, and you'll find your honeymoon much more delightful. Rather than feeling bitter that your dreams were not fulfilled, you'll be enchanted that so much turned out well.

How Long Should Your Honeymoon Last?

Try to plan at least a two-week trip, longer if you can. You need this concentrated time to get to know each other and to delight in your new relationship. Once you come back to "real life" you can never again capture this carefree time.

It's better, if you must, to stay in lower-cost cabins and prepare some meals or picnics and afford a longer trip than to go first-class for a shorter time.

Family counselor Craig Massey recommends a couple take a year-long honeymoon, based on Deuteronomy 24:5, "When a man hath taken a new wife, he shall not go out to war, neither shall he be charged with any business: but he shall be free at home one year, and shall cheer up his wife which he hath taken."

According to Massey, if a couple saved their money, then had a small, unpretentious home wedding, requesting money gifts, they could take an unhurried year to lay the foundation of their marriage. He recommends studying God's Word together to develop spiritual communication. Study nature, enjoying the changing seasons. Read and discuss a wide range of books. Develop sports and hobbies. Communicate about everything so that you know each other intimately in every area: spiritual, emotional, intellectual, and physical. Couples who have done this recommend it highly.

If you can't take a year-long honeymoon (or disagree with Massey's interpretation), adapt the principles of this Scripture. Plan for a year of adjustments. Jealously guard your time with each other by refusing extra responsibilities, such as a second job. Nor should you take on extra duties at church with committees and Sunday-school teaching. Although a worthy use of time, these should wait until after your first year. God established marriage long before He established the church. Establish spiritual depth with each other, and you'll have more to give others. You'll have the rare example of a loving marriage.

Your Vocabulary

A few phrases, used often, will keep the glow in your marriage. Learn them well, and use them whenever needed:

"I am wrong."
"I am sorry."
"Please forgive me."
"Here's what I appreciate about you."
"I love you."

28
Your New Family

As you take your husband's ring, you also take his family as your own. Now is the time to begin good relationships with your in-laws rather than fulfill the stereotyped jokes.

Determine now that your mother-in-law will be your friend. Whatever your differences, you both have one thing in common: you both love your husband. Build on that common love! Communicate frequently with your mother-in-law, letting her know the new developments in your life. As you discover endearing qualities about your husband, tell her. She'll be glad to know that all her effort in rearing him paid off.

You'll need two things from your mother-in-law: your husband's favorite recipes and a list of family birthdays. By remembering each with a card and personal note, you'll carve your place in the family.

Love your new family as dearly as you love your own. But always treat them as you would any friends who are *not* relatives. When they visit, serve them graciously. And when you visit their home, keep your company manners.

Help your husband to fit into your family by building up his good points to your parents and others. Help them to love the qualities that you love. As you discover his annoying traits, keep them your secret. If you share these with your mother or sisters, they will see only his defects without appreciating his strengths.

Your husband may criticize his family; you may not. Listen with empathy when he talks of family problems or discusses the weaknesses of those he loves. Use this time to deepen your understanding of your husband and the profound impact his family has had. But always exert caution before joining in the criticism. Remember that the river of love runs deep, and cutting remarks from an outsider (that's you!) will ultimately damage your trust in each other.

Dealing With Unasked Advice

If either set of parents offers unasked advice, listen appreciatively. Accept what you want, and ignore the rest. If they persist, state firmly but sweetly that "we'll have to discuss it and decide." Maintain the loving bonds of family continuity, but see to it that you "leave father and mother." Ask for their advice only when you genuinely want it.

Beware of loading arguments with "but my father says." Your father may be right. But using him as the voice of authority will undermine your husband's leadership. Encourage your husband to lead, and back him as he takes risks. You'll increase your respect for him—and increase his confidence.

How much time will you spend with each family? How will you spend holidays? Decide together, rather than allowing the family that exerts the most pressure to get the most of your time.

The more you learn to know and love your husband's family, the more fully you will know him. That's a rich dividend, well worth your investment!

29
Your New Home

You'll want to create a very special environment in your first home. As the two of you become one, your home should reflect both of your tastes and feel comfortable to both. If your tastes are similar, you'll probably agree on most decorating decisions. You may discover, however, that your ideas about living styles and color schemes are radically different. Begin early in your engagement to talk and window-shop until you agree on a scheme that is neither yours nor mine but ours.

How to Choose a Home

What type of first home will you have? Begin looking now to see what type of apartment or home fits your budget. Rent or house payments should not exceed 20 to 25 percent of your take-home pay, so discipline yourselves to look in your budget range. What features are the most important to you—a picturesque view, plenty of space, convenience to public transportation? Keep discussing your values and looking until you find the place that seems "just right" for both of you.

What type of space will you have? Even if you haven't signed a lease, you probably know whether you'll be living in a studio apartment, or whether you'll have a separate bedroom (or two). If it's a studio, you'll want a sofa-sleeper and small, multipurpose furniture. If you have a separate bedroom, you'll have a choice of bed sizes.

What life-style do you enjoy? Before you shop for furniture, talk together about the type of life you'll probably lead. Are you strictly casual, or do you enjoy dressing up? Choose styles that reflect your preference. Will you be doing much entertaining? Then look for an adequate kitchen and plan extra seating in the living room and buy a table that expands. Do you enjoy special hobbies? Plan work and display space. Does one of you need a quiet spot to study and relax? Then set aside a part of the living room or bedroom for a desk or make a quiet nook for reading, listening to music, or other quiet pastimes.

What colors do you enjoy? Think about the colors you have now. Do you feel comfortable, or do you yearn for something else? What colors do you usually choose for your wardrobe? Are there colors that either of you detests?

Browse through magazines, through store displays, or visit model homes until you discover what styles, colors, and moods appeal to you. Even the decor of a favorite restaurant may give you clues.

When you have some idea of the size of your first home and your tastes, begin planning your decorating scheme. List the furnishing you'll need. If either or both of you have usable furniture, you may have the nucleus for furnishing your home. Beware, however, of using any piece that one of you dislikes, or of decorating around a sofa that you plan to discard in a few years.

Your most important room will be your bedroom. Your bedroom should be a haven to you both. Avoid pink ruffles or frilly lamps. Work toward a peaceful atmosphere that is neither feminine nor masculine, but a blend of your tastes.

Wherever you must trim your budget, don't skimp on a bed. Invest in a good one. Since you will receive linens for wedding gifts, choose the size bed you'll want for several years. A standard double size may not be adequate if either of you is tall. Consider a queen, or if you have the space, a king. Or you might want a waterbed. If so, register for flat, double-size sheets which you can easily convert to fitted waterbed sheets.

How long do you expect to live in your first home? If you will be there only a year or two, invest in a few adaptable pieces of quality furniture. Spend as little as possible on curtains and other items that might not fit into your next home.

If you expect to move before long, or if you are still unsure of your tastes, consider shopping for your furnishings at garage sales, flea markets, auctions, or secondhand shops. If you have the time to invest in a bit of refinishing, you can find some great bargains. And when you're ready to move or your tastes change, you can have your own sale.

Bibliography

DURING YOUR ENGAGEMENT

Fryling, Robert and Alice. *A Handbook for Engaged Couples.* Downers Grove, Ill.: Inter-Varsity Press, 1978.

Powell, John. *Why Am I Afraid to Love?* Niles, Ill.: Argus Comm., 1972.

Small, Dwight H. *Design for Christian Marriage.* Old Tappan, N.J.: Fleming H. Revell, 1959.

Trobisch, Walter. *Love Is a Feeling to Be Learned.* Downers Grove, Ill.: Inter-Varsity Press, 1968.

BOOKS ON MARRIAGE

Chapman, Gary. *Toward a Growing Marriage.* Chicago: Moody Press, 1979.

Getz, Gene A. *The Measure of a Marriage.* Glendale, Cal.: Regal, 1980.

Mace, David and Vera. *How to Have a Happy Marriage.* Nashville: Abingdon, 1977.

Meredith, Don. *Becoming One.* Nashville: Thomas Nelson Publishers, 1979.

Schaeffer, Edith. *What Is a Family?* Old Tappan, N.J.: Fleming H. Revell, 1975.

Small, Dwight H. *After You've Said I Do.* Old Tappan, N.J.: Fleming H. Revell, 1968.

Small, Dwight H. *Your Marriage Is God's Affair.* Old Tappan, N.J.: Fleming H. Revell, 1979.

Trobisch, Walter. *I Married You.* New York: Harper and Row, 1971.

THE WEDDING DRESS

Ein, Claudia. *How to Make Your Own Wedding Gown.* New York: Doubleday, 1978.

ETIQUETTE

Ford, Charlotte. *Book of Modern Manners.* New York: Simon and Schuster, 1980.

Post, Elizabeth L. *Wedding Etiquette.* New York: Funk and Wagnalls, 1970.

Vanderbilt, Amy, revised and expanded by Letitia Baldridge. *The Amy Vanderbilt Complete Book of Etiquette.* New York: Doubleday, 1978.

COMMUNICATION

Augsburger, David. *Caring Enough to Confront.* Glendale, Cal.: Regal, 1979.

Powell, John. *Why Am I Afraid to Tell You Who I Am?* Niles, Ill.: Argus Comm., 1969.

Tournier, Paul. *To Understand Each Other.* Atlanta, Ga.: John Knox Press, 1967.

Wright, Norman H. *Communication: Key to Your Marriage.* Glendale, Cal.: Regal, 1974.

MONEY

Bowman, George M. *How to Succeed with Your Money.* Chicago: Moody Press, n.d.

Fooshee, George, Jr. *You Can Be Financially Free.* Old Tappan, N.J.: Fleming H. Revell, 1977.

Sharp, Floyd and MacDonald, Al. *Handbook for Financial Faithfulness.* Grand Rapids, Mich.: Zondervan, 1975.

Sider, Ronald. *Rich Christians in an Age of Hunger: A Biblical Study.* Downers Grove, Ill: Inter-Varsity Press, 1977.

SEX

LaHaye, Tim and Beverly. *The Act of Marriage.* Grand Rapids, Mich.: Zondervan, 1976.

Wheat, Ed and Gaye. *Intended for Pleasure.* Old Tappan, N.J.: Fleming H. Revell, 1977.